Guide to Becoming an
EFFECTIVE
MANAGER

Thoughts for Consideration

RICHARD A. PAZASIS

PAGE PUBLISHING, INC.
Conneaut Lake, PA

First originally published by Page Publishing 2019

ISBN 978-1-64701-409-4 (pbk)
ISBN 978-1-64701-410-0 (digital)

Printed in the United States of America

To my wonderful wife, Lee.
Your patience and understanding, while I climbed the
managerial ladder, was what made me so successful.
And your unequivocal support when I finally reached the
top by working long days, from early morning into the
evening, and often on weekends, can never be repaid.
And now your encouragement, to put into words
what I learned along my journey, will help others
also successfully climb the same ladder.

Preface

Upon retiring at an early age, as the result of a successful career in management (i.e., management within this guide is used as an all-encompassing term defined in the *Merriam-Webster's Dictionary and Thesaurus* as judicious use of means to accomplish an end as in directing an enterprise, as an administrator, director, executive, superintendent, supervisor) (8, para:507), it became apparent that I still have something to offer individuals who desire to become successful managers of private and public organizations. My forty years of taking management-based courses, working in various administrative positions and at different management levels within both private and public organizations, mentoring others wishing to enter the field of management, reading management-related publications, and evaluating the effectiveness of organizations as a consultant, can, even now, be worthwhile by sharing what I learned in my "thoughts for consideration" guide with those who wish to become successful managers of established and new organizations.

I extend my appreciation to the professors who had patience with me in the classroom, managers who hired and mentored me throughout my professional career, employees who contributed to my knowledge regarding how an organization really works, individuals who I mentored so they may become effective managers, and authors of numerous management-related publications who presented their theories that I experimented with while working in various management positions. I only wish to share the result of my many years of applying to real life what I learned about being an effective manager of organizations.

> The best teacher is not the one who knows the most, but the one who is most capable of reducing knowledge to that simple compound of the obvious and wonderful. (Henry Louis Mencken, American English Language Scholar)

Although all of my courses and readings related to management were useful, one course and three publications most influenced my career and contributed substantially to the writing of this guide. The course was Management of Human Behavior, Professor George A. Hill, PhD, Certificate of Special Studies Program, Harvard University. The publications were Keith Davis, PhD, *Human Behavior at Work: Organizational Behavior*, New York: McGraw-Hill Book Company, 1981; Stephen R. Covey, *The 7 Habits of Highly Effective People*, New York: Simon and Schuster, 1980; and Ronald J. Burke and Cary L. Cooper, *Building More Effective Organizations*, United Kingdom: Cambridge University Press, 2008.

Additionally, I wish to call your attention to two other publications, both cleverly written and very entertaining, that I also used to emphasize the knowledge and skills necessary to become a successful leader and manager. The publications are Wess Roberts, *Leadership Skills of Attila the Hun*, New York: Warren Books, 1989; and Eric Harvey, David Cottrell, Al Lucia, and Mike Hourigan, *The Leadership Secrets of Santa Claus*, Dallas: Performance Systems Corporation, 2003.

The following pages, in addition to the Introduction, present my "thoughts for consideration" in an easy-to-read format, with supporting quotations from authors of management-related publications, effective leaders of organizations, and other successful individuals, under the following categories related to the basic knowledge and skills necessary to become an effective manager of organizations:

1. Who you are—vital personality and value traits necessary for the effective management of an organization
2. Leadership—key elements related to the ultimate responsibility and accountability for successfully leading others to carry out the purpose and expectations of an organization
3. Organization—components related to the development and maintenance of an organization's structure and to clearly communicate its structure
4. Goals and objectives—the development of achievable goals, objectives, and strategies for an organization and to clearly communicate such goals, objectives, and strategies
5. Communication—the establishment and use of effective two-way communication throughout an organization
6. Administration—the creation of efficient procedures to ensure the most cost-effective operation of an organization, to ensure that proper fiduciary responsibilities such as legal and financial requirements are complied with, and to clearly keep records of and communicate such procedures
7. Management—the implementation of coordinated oversight to effectively support, monitor, and evaluate an organization and its employees and to clearly communicate such support, monitoring, and evaluation

Also, I have presented in *bold* lettering, throughout this guide and when appropriate, recommendations regarding important components for consideration when developing and implementing specific plans related to my "thoughts for consideration." Finally, included within this guide, there is a chart to be used to follow one's own progress toward implementing the recommended knowledge and skill necessary to become an effective manager and a bibliography listing only a few of the many published works that I have read and have used to apply management theory within real-world situations.

It should be noted that although I have presented my "thoughts for consideration" regarding what it takes to be a successful manager of a private and public organization into seven distinct knowledge and skill categories, all seven are interconnected, usually overlap, and are often dependent upon each other for a manager to be effective (i.e., just like the interconnected dependency required of employees for an organization to be successful—as in teamwork).

> There needs to be some structure that holds together the many parts of an organization so that they can become an integrated team working towards common goals. (4:245)

> The achievements of an organization are the results of the combined effort of each individual. (Vince Lombardi, "Hall of Fame" Football Coach, Green Bay Packers)

> I've always found that the speed of the boss is the speed of the team. (Lee Iacocca, Retired CEO of Chrysler Corporation)

> Talent wins games, but teamwork wins championships. (Michael Jordan, "Hall of Fame" Basketball Player, Chicago Bulls)

If you wish to become an effective manager, you need to be knowledgeable and skillful concerning your managerial strengths, at the very least, in the categories and subcategories presented within this guide, although they are not inclusive of all the managerial knowledge and skills necessary for managers to be successful. This might seem to be an overwhelming expectation, but keeping your current strengths at a high level and working to improve your weak areas, to close any gap between what you should do and what you currently don't do, should be an integral part of your ongoing professional development.

Organizations today are facing heightened challenges in their efforts to perform effectively. These challenges are reflected in the failure of many long-standing organizations and the shortened tenure of senior-level executives. There is increasing agreement that the unique competitive advantage organizations have today lies in their people, their human resource management practices and their cultures. All other elements of production can readily be obtained, bought or copied. We are now in the era of human capital; to be successful, organizations need to unleash the talents of their people. Fortunately, we now have considerable understanding of what high-performing organizations look like. However, a large gap still exists between what we know and what managers actually do. (2:First Page)

How we, as individuals, are growing and changing within our organizations is crucial to the destiny of the organization. (7:23)

Learning experiences are like journeys. The journey starts where the learning is now, and ends when the learner is successful. The end of the journey isn't knowing more, it's doing more. (Julie Dirksen, Fortune 500 Company Consultant)

You are your greatest asset. Put your time, effort and money into training, grooming, and encouraging your greatest asset. (Tom Hopkins, International Executive Training Consultant)

I hated every minute of training, but I said, "Don't quit. Suffer now and live the rest of your life as a champion." (Muhammad Ali, World Champion Boxer)

A manager's most important role, after hiring the most talented employees and providing them with the needed resources to be successful, is to continually acknowledge their effort and success with genuine appreciation. Unfortunately, the acknowledgment of appreciation is not always foremost on a manager's "things to do" list.

My own personal example to convey how important and worthwhile the use of genuine appreciation can be is as follows. Even though having been retired for over nine years as the CEO of a medium-sized organization with six different worksites, I learned that two of my former employees, both named Karen, were about to retire from one of these worksites. One, an office secretary, and the other, a nurse, spent fifteen years in my employment. I arrived at their worksite one morning with coffee and pastry. I told them how much I appreciated their skill, dedication, and loyalty while I was their CEO. They were very surprised and so appreciative that I took the time to return, long after being retired, to express my gratefulness. Within two days following my visit, I received thank-you cards with the following inscriptions:

> I would like to thank you so much for the coffee and muffins. Not only that—to go out of your way to thank us for working with you, I felt so wonderful. You made my day. I felt so appreciated. (Karen, Secretary)

> I can't tell you how appreciative I am that you took the time to come to my worksite and were so generous with your kind words. I was beaming the whole day. (Karen, Nurse)

My point is, above all else, that a successful organization is built upon the manager's understanding that the levels of skill, job implementation, and loyalty of all employees within the organization and his/her personal attention to and communication with all employees, including acknowledging and rewarding employee cooperation and performance, will always be important to its success and should constantly receive a manager's attention.

> The business environment today is more demanding than ever. To succeed…organizations need to "treat people right." Treating people right is very difficult however, with organizations and individuals having important roles. Organizations need to motivate and satisfy their employees; employees need to help make their organizations effective and peak performing. (2:21)

> To change to a peak performing organization and a fired-up workforce will make new demands of organizational leadership and raise standards for both front-line workers and managers alike. Leaders will have to be more emotional, becoming more personal, supportive and interactive. Leaders will need to unleash the emotional energy of employees. (2:11)

> Receiving recognition for achievements is one of the most fundamental of human needs. It is not childish and, rather than making employees complacent, reinforces their accomplishments, and helping to insure there will be more of them. Effective recognition should take place day-to-day and through formal programs. (2:51)

> So we focused…on producing personal and organizational excellence in an entirely different way by developing information and reward systems which reinforce the value of cooperation. (3:206)

Research indicates that employees have three prime needs: Interesting work, recognition for doing a good job, and being let in on things that are going on in the company. (Zig Ziglar, Personal Development Consultant)

Recognition is not a scarce resource. You can't use it up or run out of it. (Susan M. Heathfield, Human Resource Consultant)

If you do not treat people with respect they deserve, do not expect any kind of commitment to your productivity goals and target. (Ian Fuhr, CEO of Sorbet Group)

Before moving on, I would like to bring five important topics to the attention of those wishing to improve their managerial skills (i.e., becoming a more effective manager).

First, you need to develop and implement effective time management skills and, in doing so, learn to overcome the natural powerful pull of human nature to overcome wasting time on the job.

The challenge is not to manage time, but to manage ourselves. (4:150)

The fundamental causes of much of our problems with time can be traced to some powerful tendencies of human nature. "Practically all the rules" of time management are contradictory to the laws of human nature. (6:5)

I just didn't have enough time. Yes you did. You had all the time there is. You had the same twenty-four hours, the same 1,440 minutes, that everyone else did. What you didn't have are the skills of managing the time that's available to you. (6:3)

My favorite things in life don't cost any money. It's really clear that the most precious resource we have is time. (Steve Jobs, former CEO of Apple Inc.)

You may delay, but time will not. (Benjamin Franklin, statesman, author, scientist, one of the Founding Fathers of the United States)

It is not enough to be busy... The question is: What are we busy about? (Henry David Thoreau, American essayist and historian)

Second, every individual contemplating a management position should be aware of two debates: the first regarding whether or not leaders are born or made, and the second, how fast an individual should work his or her way up to the top spot in an organization.

A well-known and controversial debate exists regarding the importance of working one's way up through an organization to earn a management position within that organization or within a similar organization (i.e., experiencing and learning all the technical aspects of the organization) versus being brought in from outside the organization without prior experience and technical knowledge specific to the organization (i.e., born with talents reinforced only by classroom education). There exist examples of individuals who worked their way up the ladder of an organization, both with and without formal management education and training, some who were successful and some who were not successful. And there also are examples of both successful and unsuccessful managers with formal management education and training who have been brought in from the outside to manage without any experience directly within the organization or without the specific technical knowledge base that supports the type of organization they will enter. In my opinion, the most effective managers acquire both the specific technical knowledge base and adequate related on-the-job experience by climbing the ladder in their current or similar type of organization while at the same time acquiring formal classroom management theory and practice.

> Tell me and I'll forget. Show me and I may remember. Involve me and I'll understand. The evidence is clear that most leadership development occurs through what is variously referred to as action learning, experimental learning, on-the-job learning, or learning by doing. (2:133)

> The most dangerous leadership myth is that leaders are born—that there is a genetic factor in leadership. This myth asserts that people simply have certain charismatic qualities or not. That's nonsense; in fact, the opposite is true. Leaders are made rather than born. (Warren G. Bennis, Leadership Consultant and Author)

> Most wisdom is gained by experiencing different things (compared to acquiring knowledge through schooling or other means)… Experience is the best teacher after all. (Farlex Dictionary 2015)

> You will learn more from things that happen to you in real life than you will from hearing about it or studying things that happen to other people. I don't care how many books you read about how to run a business; experience is the best teacher. (McGraw-Hill Dictionary 2002)

But the debate regarding how quickly an individual in management moves up the ladder, into the top leadership position of an organization, is far less discussed among experts. In my opinion, based on forty years of formal education and experience within various levels of management, I feel that being patient and taking one's time to climb that tall ladder will ultimately pay larger dividends regarding your ultimate success when in the leadership chair. The more time spent in various management positions will significantly increase your contact with a variety of management experiences, which will make all the difference in your ability to successfully mature as a manager (i.e., develop the appropriate knowledge and skills through trial and error) and make your goal of becoming and retaining the "top dog" position in an organization attainable.

> According to many long-term research studies, the optimal mix of learning methodologies to develop skills to become an effective leader is something in the neighborhood of: 70% from work experiences, 20% from other people, and 10% from coursework. (2:133)

> "Leadership development does not happen overnight." Building leadership is a process. This process is followed strictly in most global international companies. Every organization starts with a pool of talent… The next step is to make sure that people get the right opportunities. One thing we do is train people properly. In the next five to seven years after the initial steps, you start looking at the individual's ability to deal with relationships… The role of the organization is to create a pool whose members can occupy various positions in the organization. Leaders evolve from within as the organization grows. (K. V. Kamath, CEO of New Development Bank; *Business Today*, para: January 5, 2014)

> Mastering a skill can take years or, as Malcolm
> Gladwell, of the ILR School at Cornell University
> says, 10,000 hours. Leadership is a skill that can
> be taught and developed. Unfortunately, it is a
> difficult one to master… After years of research
> and personal experience, I have never been more
> convinced that leadership is a journey and not a
> destination. (John Eades, CEO of LearnLoft)

Third, I cannot stress enough the importance of understanding and controlling the implementation of technology as a manager.
Everyone is aware of the value that technology has contributed to the
success of organizations. Both hardware and software development,
over a very short period of time, have helped organizations become
extremely efficient and effective. Whether it be the collection, storage, analysis, and publication of information or more sophisticated
uses such as wireless communication, robotic manufacturing including 3-D printing, self-driving vehicles, and the development of
advanced artificial intelligence capabilities, technology continues to
be a necessary component of any successful organization. However,
there is the danger that technology could evolve to such a level that it
will replace all human interpersonal interactions necessary to manage
a successful organization.

> Technology is moving so fast that it is creating
> social problems long before society is able to
> develop solutions. (4:264)

> As our knowledge of computers becomes more
> sophisticated, the hardware more accessible, the
> operation less costly, and the service more effi-
> cient, our reliance upon the machine moves
> toward an unhealthy dependency. (7:62)

> Technology is a useful servant but a danger-
> ous master. (Christian Louis Lange, Norwegian
> Scientist)

> It has become appallingly obvious that our
> technology has exceeded our humanity. (Albert
> Einstein, "Nobel Prize" Theoretical Physicist)

> Old robots are becoming more human and young
> humans are becoming more like robots. (Lorin
> Morgan-Richards, children's literature author)

Dan Brown, in his number 1 worldwide best seller *Origin* (1), brought to his readers attention what has and will continue to happen regarding what he calls "This new species.... It expands its territory continuously. And most importantly, it evolves…must faster than humans do" (1:562).

> Consider this… It took early humans over a
> million years to progress from discovering fire
> to inventing the wheel. Then it took only a few
> thousand years to invent the printing press.
> Then it took only a couple hundred years to
> build a telescope. In the centuries that followed,
> in ever-shortening spans, we bounded from the
> steam engine, to gas-powered automobiles, to the
> Space Shuttle. And then, it took only two decades
> for us to start modifying our own DNA! (1:133)

Dan Brown goes on to imply that the human race will be swallowed up by this new species over the next few decades (1:564). He already sees, as do we: "images of people clutching cell phones, wearing virtual-reality goggles, adjusting Bluetooth devices in their ears, runners with music players strapped to their arms…" (1:568). And he warns us that this is just the beginning.

We are now starting to embed computer chips into our brains, inject our blood with tiny cholesterol-eating nanobots that live in us forever, build synthetic limbs that are controlled by our minds, use genetic editing tools like CRISPR to modify our genome, and quite literally, engineer an enhanced version of ourselves. (1:568)

To finally bring my point home, regarding the importance of avoiding the potential of technology distancing ourselves from and even replacing all human interpersonal interactions necessary to manage a successful organization, I would like to tell you about a recent television commercial that I watched with great interest.

A young boy, perhaps a third grader, is sitting at the dinner table with his mother to his right-hand side of the table and his father to his left-hand side. The young lad evidently had a wonderful day in school and begins to tell his parents about his day. While he is enthusiastically telling his story, both his parents are holding their smartphones and texting. The young boy becomes frustrated because his parents are not really paying attention. He smiles at his parents and explains that his class is going on a field trip to Mars, and he will need his permission slip signed. At which time, his father says that he will sign the permission slip following dinner and offers to be a chaperone on the trip if there is room for him. Need I say more!

Fourth, despite how well prepared you are to lead and manage an organization, you will never be without experiencing the stress of having to make difficult decisions. In the words of Ralph Waldo Emerson, American essayist, poet, and lecturer, "Whatever course you decide upon, there is always someone to tell you that you are wrong. There are always difficulties arising, which tempt you to believe that your critics are right. To map out a course of action and follow it to an end requires courage." You need to accept the fact that organizations and the environment surrounding them continue to become more complex, and wherever there are people, there will be problems; there will be conflict. Therefore, work stress creates significant human dilemmas, especially at the executive levels of management. "Executives need special support for their work-related well-being" (2:87). Setting aside time to keep yourself physically fit, taking periodic vacations, and wisely utilizing leisure time should be high on your list to help manage stress. And if these fixes are not sufficient, seeking professional counseling help should be considered. You should learn through experience, despite the risks, to take decision-making head-on. Even making bad decisions can be beneficial.

> According to the American Institute of Stress, work stress may well have reached epidemic proportions… Therefore, work stress clearly qualifies as a significant organizational challenge for worker, for their leaders, and for their executives. (2:84)

> Organizations are not static. They either grow or they deteriorate. Conflict is an ingredient of growth. (7:73)

> Within certain limits we make choices among an array of options; it's an inviolate aspect of our heritage. Making a choice is an act, and acts have consequences. (7:43)

> What we do with our leisure may benefit our organization. (7:109)

> Every decision involves some risk. It is unfortunate when final decisions are made by chieftains headquartered miles from the front, where they can only guess at conditions and potentialities known only to the captain on the battlefield. (10, para:103–104)

You can't always control what goes on outside, but you can always control what goes on inside. (Wayne Dyer, self-help author and consultant)

The more we run from conflict, the more it masters us; the more we try to avoid it, the more it controls us; the less we fear conflict, the less it confuses us; the less we deny our differences, the less they divide us. (David Augsburger, author, counselor, and minister)

Fifth, it is difficult, today, to comprehend why some individuals in management positions fail to apply effective practices based on proven research and theory. There certainly are enough management courses and literature available for any person wishing to become an effective manager to take advantage of and utilize. However, it seems that there is a pervasive indifference to applying best management practices and theory, due to either personal laziness (i.e., not taking the courses, reading the literature, applying proven management practices) or allowing the newly acquired power of becoming a manger "to go to one's head." And so one keeps on doing the same ineffective thing over and over again.

Too many organizations are wedded to outdated HRM [human resource management] practices that are out of step with the demands of today's business environment. (2:1)

Managers are generally unaware of practices that work effectively and seem uninterested in finding out about them. (2:28)

We, and our organizations, tend to settle for less than we are and could be. (7:14)

We learn only when we want to learn. (7:27)

The definition of insanity is doing the same thing over and over again, but expecting different results. (Albert Einstein, "Nobel Prize" theoretical physicist)

If your only tool is a hammer, then every problem looks like a nail. (Abraham Maslow, former psychologist, university professor, researcher, and author)

Power is the ultimate aphrodisiac. (Henry Kissinger, secretary of state and "Nobel Prize" recipient)

Even the smallest dose of power can change a person. You've seen it. Someone gets promoted or a bit of fame and then…. (NPR Radio Broadcast, August 10, 2013, "On Research," by Wilfrid Laurier, former Canadian prime minister)

To conclude, my intention for writing this guide was to offer individuals who wish to become effective managers of private and public organizations my own "thoughts for consideration" in a very simple easy-to-read format rather than in a several hundred-page textbook that commonly contains numerous charts, formulas, graphs, and theories regarding management practices, which are often presented in a most complex manner. In addition, I intentionally use, or in fact overuse, quotations to drive home my "thoughts for consideration," so there is no doubt how each thought relates to effective management and the success of organizations.

In our time-starved and information-overloaded culture, most of us have far too little time to read. As a result, our understanding of important subjects often tend to float on the surface—without insights of writings from thinkers and teachers who have spent years studying these subjects. (9:Preface)

If you have an important point to make, don't try to be subtle or clever. Use a pile driver. Hit the point once. Then come back and hit it again. Then hit it a third time—a tremendous whack. (Winston Churchill, former British prime minister)

Best wishes for reaching your goal to become an effective manager.

Introduction

Many years ago, during my first session of a course on the management of organizations, the professor entered the classroom after all his students were seated. He wrote on the chalkboard, "What is an organization?" And then he immediately asked for the definition of an organization. Several hands went up, and to his dismay, all the definitions seemed to be very long and complicated. He then wrote on the chalkboard, "KIS = Keep It Simple." His students became silent. The professor went on to state, "If only one person is needed to reach a goal, there is no organization. However, if two or more individuals are needed to reach a goal (i.e., resulting in a social institution), then you have an organization." He finally wrote on the chalkboard, "An organization: two or more human beings working together to reach a goal." He went on to say, "The more individuals required to reach a goal, the more complex the organization, and the more structure is required to coordinate human interactions and motivation. Therefore, the manager of an organization must understand social systems and the individual differences, needs, and value systems of human beings, as well as how to motivate people."

> Organization: an association of persons having a common interest. (Merriam-Webster's Dictionary and Thesaurus; 8:587)

> Organizations are social systems. If one wishes to work in them or to manage them, it is necessary

to understand how they operate. Organizations combine science and people... There are no simple cookbook formulas for working with people... We can work effectively with people if we are prepared to think about them in human terms. (4:2)

Organizational behavior is the study and application of knowledge about how people act within an organization... The key elements in organizational behavior are people, structure, technology, and the external environment in which the organization operates. When people join together in an organization to accomplish an objective, some kind of structure is required. (4:3–4)

The manager of any private or public organization needs to understand the fundamentals of his/her organization, its formal and social systems, and the individual differences, needs, and value systems of human beings, as well as how to motivate people to successfully do their jobs (i.e., get things done) to reach his/her organization's goals.

There is increasing agreement that the unique competitive advantage organizations have today lies in their people, their human resource management practices and systems and their cultures.
The past decade has produced research evidence supporting the critical role that people play in the success of organizations. (2:Preface)

Whether he works in a business...in a governmental agency...the executive is, first of all, expected to get the right things done. (Peter F. Drucker, American management consultant)

Every company has two organizational structures: The formal one is written on the charts; the other is the everyday relationship of the men and women in the organization. (Harold S. Geneen, retired president of ITT)

Leadership is the ability to facilitate movement in the needed direction and have people feel good about it. (Tom Smith, cofounder of Partners In Leadership)

If you want something to happen, you have to make people able and you have to make them want to. (Steve Kerr, CLO of Goldman Sachs)

You get the job done or you don't. (Bill Belichick, head NFL coach, New England Patriots)

And why present this guide in a very focused, succinct, and easy-to-read format rather than in a long and complex narrative usually found in most management-related published works? Because of two valuable pieces of knowledge that I took away from my course on Effective Business Writing in the Certificate of Special Studies Program at Harvard, which were to be as direct as possible regarding what I want to communicate (e.g., using a bullet-like or outline format when possible) and always reducing the number of words used to as few as possible while still getting my intent across to the readers (referred to by my professor as reducing the "lard factor"). In addition, my outline can be easily presented in a checklist format, also included within this guide, for one's use to chart out, track, and evaluate one's implementation of my "thoughts for consideration."

The more elaborate our means of communication, the less we communicate. (Joseph Priestley, English philosopher)

> Communicate unto the other person that which
> you would want him to communicate unto you
> if your positions were reversed. (Aaron Goldman,
> professor of communication, Harvard University)

Hopefully, the following sections of this guide, through my "thoughts for consideration" presented in an easy-to-read outline format, will assist and mentor those individuals seeking to become effective managers of private and public organizations.

Who You Are

Your genuine character (i.e., personal traits), core values, and natural talents, which are brought to any managerial position, or who you are, will be vital as the foundation to successfully managing any organization.

Character is the foundation of Win/Win, and everything else builds on that foundation. (3:217)

As my study took me back through 200 years of about success, I noticed a startling pattern emerging in the content of the literature... I began to feel more and more that much of the success literature of the past 50 years was superficial. It was filled with social image consciousness, techniques and quick fixes—with social band-aids and aspirin that addressed acute problems and sometimes even appeared to solve them temporarily (Personality Ethic), but left the underlying chronic problems to fester and resurface time and again.

In stark contrast, almost all the literature in the first 150 years or so focused on what could be called the Character Ethic as the foundation of success—things like integrity, humility, fidelity, temperance, courage, justice, patience, industry, simplicity, modesty, and the Golden Rule.

The Character Ethic taught that there are basic principles of effective living, and that people can only experience true success and enduring happiness as they learn and integrate these principles into their basic character. (3:18)

Leadership consists not in degrees of techniques, but in traits of character. (Lewis H. Lapham, editor, *Harper's Magazine*)

Be more concerned with your character than your reputation, because your character is what you really are, while your reputation is merely what others think you are. (John Wooden, "Hall of Fame" head basketball coach, UCLA)

Although it is true that an individual can learn how to be a more effective manager, supported by the vast number of managerial science courses, management internship programs, and publications in management and leadership, which exist to improve performance, you will have a better proclivity toward consistent and long-term management effectiveness if you truly exhibit certain character traits and have specific core values that are intrinsic to your demeanor.

But shortly after World War I the view of success shifted from the Character Ethic to...the Personality Ethic. Success became more a function of personality, of public image, of attitudes and behaviors, skills and techniques that lubricate the processes of human interaction.

Other parts of the personality approach were clearly manipulative, even deceptive, encouraging people to use techniques to get other people to like them, or to fake interest in the hobbies of others to get out of them what they wanted, or to use the "power look," or to intimidate their way through life.

Some...literature acknowledged character as an ingredient of success, but tended to compartmentalize it rather than recognize it as a foundational and catalytic. Reference to the Character Ethic became mostly lip service; the basic thrust was quick-fix influence techniques, power strategies, communication skills, and positive attitudes. (3:19)

Character is like a tree and reputation is like a shadow. The shadow is what we think of it; the tree is the real thing. (Abraham Lincoln, sixteenth president of the United States)

Character is the indelible mark that determines the only true value of all people and all their work. (Orison Swett Marden, American author and *Success Magazine* founder)

Character cannot be developed in ease and quiet. Only through experience of trial and suffering can the soul be strengthened, vision cleared, ambition inspired, and success achieved. (Helen Keller, 1964 Medal of Freedom Recipient and 1965 Women's "Hall of Fame")

In my opinion, in other opinions by experts in the field of management science such as Stephen R. Covey, and also subscribed to by Wess Roberts in his creative publication of *Leadership Secrets of Attila the Hun* (10:16–22), character traits and core values should be consistently exhibited in any management position, which include the following:

1. Self-confidence: to have strong feelings of assurance to meet challenges. If you do not have and maintain the confidence that you can meet challenges, then you will rely too much on luck and will experience failure. Self-confidence will give you resiliency in any management position to overcome the misfortunes, rejections, and disappointments that everyone experiences in life.

    Those who portray a lack of self-confidence in their abilities to carry out leadership assignments give signs to their subordinates, peers and superiors that [their] duties are beyond their capabilities. (10:20)

    You must have resilience to overcome personal misfortunes, discouragement, rejection and disappointment. (10:26)

    Have confidence that if you have done a little thing well, you can do a bigger thing well too. (Joseph Story, Former United States Supreme Court Justice)

    When someone tells me no, it doesn't mean I can't do it, it simply means I can't do it with him. (Karen E. Quinones Miller, African American journalist)

    Success is often achieved by those who don't know that failure is inevitable. (Coco Chanel, French fashion designer and Chanel Perfume brand founder)

2. Courage: to fearlessly accept inherent risks when attempting to overcome obstacles and while fulfilling responsibilities. If you do not develop courage, you may often become bewildered and disconnected in the face of adversities and losses. Courage will allow you to press on despite any fear and ultimately achieve at high levels.

    Chieftains who lead Huns must have courage. They must be fearless and have the fortitude to carry out assignments given them—the gallantry to accept the risks of leadership. They must not balk at obstacles, nor must they become bewildered when in the presence of adversity. (10:17)

    Too often, the leadership of many nations falls to princes who lack ambition, courage and capabilities to reign as leaders. Such disinterest, cowardice and incompetence is manifested in various actions that discourage and bewilder subordinates, thus strengthening the enemy. (10:25)

    I love the man that can smile in trouble, that can gather strength from distress, and can grow brave by reflections. (Thomas Paine, American philosopher)

    Courage is being scared to death, but saddling up anyway. (John Wayne, American actor)

    To uncover your true potential, you must first find your own limits and then have the courage to blow past them. (Picabo Street, Olympic Gold Medalist Ski Racer)

3. Emotional and Physical Stamina: to have the wherewithal (mental/physical health and endurance) to recover from

both short-term and longer-term challenges and even failures. Lacking emotional and physical stamina often leads to distorted viewpoints, a loss of a clear perspective to accomplish goals, and the lack of physical energy that will keep you from leading the charge and recovering quickly from small defeats so you can win the big ones.

We must ensure that our leaders at every level have the stamina to recover rapidly from disappointment—to bounce back from discouragement, to carry out the responsibilities of their office without becoming distorted in their views—without losing clear perspective, as well as the emotional strength to persist in the face of seemingly difficult circumstances.

Huns must have chieftains who can endure the physical demands of their leadership duties. Chieftains must nurture their bodies... Chieftains cannot lead from their bedside... Our Chieftains must be strong in body in order to lead the charge. (10:18)

Let me remind you that it is only by working with an energy which is superhuman and which looks...like insanity that we can accomplish anything worth the achievement. (Woodrow Wilson, twenty-eighth president of the United States)

Mental toughness is many things and rather difficult to explain. Its qualities are sacrifice and self-denial. Also, most importantly, it is combined with a perfectly disciplined will that refuses to give in. It's a state of mind—you could call it character in action. (Vince Lombardi, "Hall of Fame" football coach, Green Bay Packers)

Grit is that "extra something" that separates the most successful people from the rest. It's the passion, perseverance, and stamina that we must channel in order to stick with our dreams until they become a reality. (Travis Bradberry, president of TalentSmart)

4. Dependability: to always let others know that they can count on you and that you trust them as team members, which is often described as credibility, honesty, integrity, and loyalty. Lacking dependability will make you a risk and not to be trusted. You do not live or work in isolation, and being dependable will allow you to more frequently accomplish goals with others through mutual trust and teamwork.

Chieftains must be credible. Their words must be believable… They must be trusted to have the intelligence and integrity to provide correct information. Leaders lacking in credibility will not gain proper influence and are to be hastily removed from positions of responsibility, for they cannot be trusted.

If a chieftain cannot be depended upon in all situations to carry out his roles and responsibilities, relieve him of them. (10: 20–21)

Dependability is more important than talent. Dependability is a talent, and it is a talent all can have. It makes no difference how much ability we possess if we are not responsible and dependable. (Floyd L. Bennett, Medal of Honor aviator)

If your actions don't live up to your words, you have nothing to say. (DaShanne Stokes, respected sociologist and social justice author)

Ability is a wonderful thing, but its value is greatly enhanced by dependability. Ability implies repeatability and accountability. (Robert A. Heinlein, American Aeronautical Engineer and Author)

5.   Empathy: to always appreciate, understand, and be sensitive toward others and to accept unique differences in others. Having empathy, and even some humbleness and humility in understanding that you are no better than anyone else, develops a stewardship within oneself that attracts others and that elicits support for one's own success from members of the integrated society that we live in.

Chieftains must develop empathy—an appreciation for an understanding of the values of others, a sensitivity for other cultures, beliefs and traditions. (10:19)

A nation of one ancestry and race is weak. We must hold strong our custom of welcoming foreigners who seek to join our cause, treating them with dignity and respect and teaching them our language and customs.
     Our accepted differences and diversities must be pooled into a common purpose worthy of our efforts as tribes and as a nation. (10:33)

No one cares how much you know, until they know how much you care. (Theodore Roosevelt, twenty-sixth president of the United States)

When you show deep empathy toward others, their defensive energy goes down, and positive energy replaces it. That is when you can get more creative in solving problem. (Stephen Covey,

1996 *Time* Magazine Top 25 Most Influential People and author of *The 7 Habits of Highly Effective People*)

Empathy is about standing in someone else's shoes, feeling with his or her heart, seeing with his or her eyes. Not only is empathy hard to outsource and automate, but it makes the world a better place. (Daniel H. Pink, *New York Times* best seller author of works related to behavioral science and business)

6.   Determination, Persistence, and Hard Work: to always maintain a sustained willingness and momentum to work hard to persevere toward and reach goals; to have a winning drive. Often, the reluctance to work hard is the most common cause of failure. Calvin Coolidge, our Twenty-Ninth President of the United States, once stated, "You may have genius, you may have talent, and you may have education, but without persistence and determination, you will not truly be successful."

Few Huns will sustain themselves without a strong personal desire…. (10:18)

An essential quality of leadership is an intrinsic desire to win. (10:19)

You've got to get up every morning with determination if you're going to go to bed with satisfaction. (George Horace Lorimer, Editor of *Saturday Evening Post* Magazine)

Construct your determination with Sustained Effort, Controlled Attention, and Concentrated Energy. Opportunities never come to those who wait… They are captured by those who dare to attack. (Paul J. Meyer, CEO of Success Motivation Institute)

I've always found that anything worth achieving will always have obstacles in the way and you've got to have that drive and determination to overcome those obstacles on route to whatever it is that you want to accomplish. (Chuck Norris, champion of Black Belt Martial Artist and American actor)

In four-time Pulitzer Prize recipient Robert Frost's famous poem "The Road Not Taken" (11:270), he describes a traveler walking through the woods. The traveler comes upon two paths and realizes that he or she can only take one path to reach his or her destination. One path is bent in undergrowth and obviously will be a challenge to navigate. The other is very smooth and a much better choice. Well, the traveler takes the more difficult path, or in Robert Frost's own words, "The one less traveled by, And that has made all the difference."

As inferred from reading this Robert Frost poem, your future journey through management positions will be challenging but to go forth with a solid foundation of self-confidence, courage, emotional stamina, dependability, empathy, and determination, persistence, and hard work, which will significantly increase your level of success as a manager within any organization.

Leadership

Leadership means having ultimate responsibility and accountability for successfully carrying out the purpose (i.e., mission) and expectations (i.e., goals) of an organization by selecting, training, supporting, motivating, and steering employees in a direction that creates and sustains a successful organization.

These [successful] organizations had magnetic leaders, a compelling legacy, and held bold, impossible dreams. Their leaders provided an inspiring vision, made all employees feel valued, and worked hard at selecting the right people. (2:8)

Leadership deals with the top line: What are the things I want to accomplish? In the words of both Peter Drucker and Warren Bennis, "Management is doing things Right; leadership is doing the right things." (3:101)

Leadership is a part of management...but all we ask of leaders is that they influence others to follow. Without leadership, an organization is only a confusion of people and machines. Leadership is the ability to persuade others to seek defined objectives enthusiastically. It is the human factor that binds a group together and motivates it towards goals. (4, para:124)

I am, after all, running a business here. I'm a boss. I've got responsibilities—both to the gift-getters and the gift-makers. There are workers to lead, letters to read, orders to fill, processes to manage, stuff to buy, stuff to make, standards to maintain, new technologies to adopt, skills to develop, elf problems to solve, and reindeer droppings to scoop (although I delegate that one). Trust me, I've got some big and not-always-easy boots to fill. (5:7)

Leadership is the privilege to have the responsibility to direct the actions of others in carrying out the purpose of the organization, at varying levels of authority and with accountability for both successful and failed endeavors. (10-xiv)

Being a leader is a privilege, and effective leadership requires not only having special attitudes, knowledge, and skills but the ability to get things done through others by using encouragement and praise (i.e., motivation) and without always being the center of attention and constantly "stealing the limelight." The most effective leaders often work quietly behind the scenes to ensure the success of their organization and bestow such success on their employees. "At times the appropriate leadership action is to stay in the background keeping pressure off the group, to keep quiet so that others may talk, to be calm in times of uproar, to hesitate, and to delay decisions" (4:125). During my career as a CEO, I have been very fortunate to have worked for talented board members, including outstanding board chairpersons. They have always been extremely caring, intelligent, and focused on our organization's mission. Recently, I received a telephone call from one of my former board chairs. She travels most of the year around the country as a nationally recognized consultant and workshop presenter for the arts. She informed me that she was back in town and would love to meet for breakfast, just to catch up. Well, it turned out to be a wonderful breakfast get-together! And the very next day, I received the following e-mail from her: "You coming to our organization certainly paid off for us. You brought to it a very special kind of leadership. Quiet, but strong. Able to listen and open to ideas. You fostered excellence and community simultaneously. They really were the good old days!"

> Senior executives in the good-to-great companies invest in building the company and not themselves. (2:13)

> Managers represent the administrative system or management system, and their role is to use organizational behavior to improve people-organization relationships... Managers try to build a climate in which people are motivated, work together, and become more effective persons. (4:5)

> You can't possibly focus on your mission without also focusing on the folks that make your mission happen. The two go hand-in-hand... And besides, since you manage things and lead people, common sense suggests that it's people who are at the core of all leadership activities. (5:14)

> Both a concern for performance and a concern for people are essential. A highly adaptive organization is characterized by managers who serve, equally well, both the corporate and collegial functions. (7:20)

> A leader is best when he is neither seen nor heard... (7:98)

Important components to consider when developing an initial implementation plan for the motivation of employees should include the following: (1) Make your business a pleasant, functional, and well-kept place to be. (2) Be a respectful, honest, and supportive manager. (3) Offer rewards such as incentive programs, bonuses, profit sharing, paying for special training, and special job titles. (4) Allow room for growth through advancement opportunities. (5) Share positive and encouraging feedback regarding their input both one-on-one and at group meetings. (6) Be transparent by sharing information about the organization on a regular basis and soliciting, accepting, and using feedback for improvements. (7) When possible, implement flexible work schedules such as flextime, partial work hours from home, and other creative scheduling options. (8) Provide free food and beverages during work hours as a daily appreciation offering. (9) Use recognition and praise for a job well done when deserved, including when they work extra hours or help a coworker. 10) Ask, from time to time, what they feel is most important to help make the organization successful (para, Victor Lipman, Author of Research Study on Employee Motivation: "What Motivates Employees to 'Go the Extra Mile,'" Mind of the Manager Publication, December 5, 2014).

Leadership can be very exciting and rewarding, but it can also cause much stress and be very draining at times. Leadership needs to result in visible achievements, sometimes against challenging and sometimes insurmountable odds, that are recognized by employees. Therefore, it is not easy being a leader.

> Work stress clearly qualifies as a significant organizational challenge for workers, for their leaders, and for their executives. (2:84)

> Executives need special support for their work-related well-being. A major reason for this is that these persons are called upon in open-ended

ways to serve other employees and the organization. (2:87)

Believe you me, having to smile and be jolly
every day when you're wearing the same thick,
red-wool suit that itches like crazy is no picnic.
(5:6)

It is soon after a new chieftain is appointed that
he will either grow or diminish in the eyes of his
subordinates, peers, and superiors. If he is prudent in the application of his authority, demon-
strates a spirit of commitment and sees that all
obligations are met, the chieftain will enlarge his
stature. Then, he will have gained personal loyalty, trust, confidence and respect from all the
Huns under his command, from his peers and
superiors. (10:97–98)

Important components to consider when developing an
implementation plan for the initial and immediate awareness of
the general attributes required to become an effective manager,
until being able to develop a more solid and long-lasting knowledge and skill base as the result of studying and practicing management practices based on proven research and theory, should
include the following: (1) Know your organization's vision and
major goals and make certain that all employees also know
the vision and main goals. 2) Be both physically and mentally
accessible to employees. (3) Be considerate of employee needs.
(4) Provide employees with the training, tools, resources, and
feedback required for success. (5) Keep employees in the "what's
happening" information loop. (6) Help employees maintain an
appropriate balance between their professional and personal
lives. (7) Demonstrate respect for employees' time and talents
as well as respect for them as individuals. (8) Help employees
develop in their jobs and also have opportunities to advance

within the organization. (9) Fairly distribute the work and workload. (10) Make certain that all employees understand the behaviors and performance outcomes that are expected to meet the organization's vision and main goals and implement effective evaluations of all employees based on the vision and main goals (5, para:12–17).

Here are some thoughts for consideration as to what helps make an effective leader:

1. To be visible and visibly proud of your organization, both internally and externally, and to be its number one cheerleader

   Research shows a strong correlation between pride in the organization and the overall satisfaction of workers with that organization. (2:47)

   I am extremely proud of the workshop that the elves, reindeer, and I have created—and we are more than happy to show it off... Yes, we do run a productive and happy place here. And that's in spite of the intense pressures and challenges we face... (5:12)

   Attila's presence was felt wherever he rode or rested. He was not only a Hun, he was the most distinguished Hun of all... He was, after all, their leader... (10:50)

   I, Attila, King of the Huns, have called this assembly of chieftains and mighty warriors together for the purpose of encouragement. Further, my aim is to kindle the fires of your emotional stamina so that you may not become hopeless in the face of disappointment. (10:87)

There's a lot of pride that business owners have. It's actually really critical that pride and ownership extends to everyone in the organization. I think of everyone in the same boat is driving the company forward. (Aaron Levie, American entrepreneur and CEO of Box Cloud)

Organization pride is stronger for employees if they believe management listens to them and if their co-workers respect them. (Bruce L. Katcher, industrial/organizational psychologist)

Organizational pride is a win-win for everyone. Pride is a catalyst for focusing on task, effort, and persistence. And it spurs us on to help others, creating powerful and uplifting feelings of connectedness and belonging, all of which build happiness at work. (Jessica Pryce-Jones, author of *Happiness at Work*)

Important components to consider when developing an implementation plan for being visible and being the organization's number one cheerleader should include the following: (1) Publish both internal and external publications regarding the accomplishments of the organization on a periodic basis. (2) Provide regular press releases containing the organization's successes. (3) Develop videos for both external and internal use that highlight the organization's successes. (4) When in public, always stress the positives (i.e., any negatives should always be kept in-house where they are best resolved). (5) Schedule periodic group and one-on-one meetings to convey your appreciation for and pride in all employee contributions and accomplishments (Richard A. Pazasis, Retired Executive and Author of *Guide to Becoming an Effective Manager: Thoughts for Consideration*).

2. To consistently convey your organization's vision, mission, and goals through writings, at meetings, during presentations, and when making decisions

Although leaders have many roles in which they must excel, creating a vision and transforming that vision into strategy is central to their position. Vision is important because it is necessary to have a clearly defined road map (core values and purpose) for a company to achieve competitive advantage. As Jack Welsh (i.e., former CEO of General Electric) asserts, "good business leaders create a vision, articulate the vision, passionately own the vision, and relentlessly drive it to completion." (2:219)

I've made it a core component of our decision-making and work-planning process. If an action we're considering doesn't support our mission, either directly or indirectly, we don't do it. (5:13)

The very essence of leadership is that you have a vision. It's got to be a vision that you articulate clearly and forcefully at every occasion. You can't blow a weak trumpet. (Theodore Hesburgh, former president of Notre Dame University)

Leadership is the capacity to translate vision into reality. (Warren G. Bennis, American organizational consultant)

Leadership is having a compelling vision, a comprehensive plan, relentless implementation, and talented people working together. (Alan Mulally, former CEO of Ford Motor Company)

Important components to consider when developing an implementation plan for conveying your organization's vision, mission, and goals should include the following: (1) making sure that all the elves and reindeer know what our mission is and why it's important; (2) keeping the mission "in front of folks" by posting it on walls, discussing it at staff meetings and training sessions, including it in internal correspondence, and through a host of other activities that help ensure it stays our central focal point; and (3) making it a core component of our decision-making and work-planning process so if an action we're considering doesn't support our mission, either directly or indirectly, we don't do it (5, para:13).

3. To spend time communicating effectively, with both employees and clients and within both the formal and informal social structures of the organization (i.e., be visible and practice effective two-way communication) so all involved with the organization will feel like partners and continually link with, contribute toward, and support the successful achievement of the organization

We emphasize that leaders need to communicate effectively... As part of their study, Beer and Eisenstat found that the quality of information and communication flowing from leaders to followers could have significant impact on whether an organization would (or could) learn. Employees need to have current and up-to-date information... (2, para:218–219)

Organizations cannot exist without communication. If there is no communication, employees cannot know what their associates are doing, management cannot receive information inputs, and management cannot give instructions. Coordination of work is impossible, and the organization will collapse for lack of it. Cooperation also becomes impossible, because people cannot communicate their needs and feelings to others. We can say with some confidence that every act of communication influences the organization in some way. (4:399)

The grapevine is the communication system of informal organization. It coexists with management's formal communication system. Although informal systems bring problems, they also bring a number of benefits for employees... Most important is the fact that they blend with formal systems to make an effective total system. Formal plans and policies cannot meet every problem in a dynamic situation because they are preestablished and partly inflexible. (4, para:333–335)

The single biggest problem in communication is the illusion that it has taken place. (George Bernard Shaw, Irish playwright)

Any problem, big or small...always seems to start with bad communication. Someone isn't listening. (Emma Thompson, British actress, screenwriter, and author)

Take advantage of every opportunity to practice your communication skills so that when important occasions arise, you will have the gift, the style, the sharpness, the clarity, and the emotions to affect other people. (Jim Rohn, American entrepreneur and author)

Important components to consider when developing an implementation plan for the development of effective two-way

communication channels should include the following: (1) Regarding downward communication, *get informed* (try to know in advance what employees and clients want to know or let them know that you will get them the answer as soon as possible), *develop positive attitude* (you need to always show that you care about communication), *plan all communication* (be sure that communication is planned ahead to ensure that it is received by employees and clients who will be the most affected by it), and *develop trust* (the development of trust through leadership's honesty and history of consistent accurate communication enhances the acceptance and accurate understanding of all communication). (2) Concerning upward communication, *encourage input* (honest and accurate upward communication will only work when it is consistently encouraged, accepted, and used by leadership), *avoid short circuits* (prevent filtering and the skipping of steps within the communication chain so only accurate information flows upward and no one in the established communication hierarchy is left out), *convey quick responses* (leaders need to respond as soon as possible to upward communication so that future communications will continue and employees and clients will see results from their input), and *upward practices* (allowing for various communication channels such as scheduled input meetings, an open door policy, and suggestion boxes for anonymous input) (4, para:422–430).

4. To be accessible, considerate, respectful, and supportive to all constituents (i.e., employees and clients) and develop positive relationships and perceptions through consistent communication and modeling by treating people right, keeping promises, standing for what is right in decision-making, and always telling the truth

    Treating people right produces long-term gains for both the organization and individuals. Organizations that "treat people right" can attract more qualified employees, retain them, and motivate them to perform at higher levels. Employees receive more interesting and challenging work, higher rewards, more varied career options and identify more with a winning organization. (2:21)

Managers represent the administrative system or management system, and their role is to use organizational behavior to improve people-organizational relationships. Managers try to build a climate in which people are motivated, work together, and become more effective persons. (4:5)

Dear Santa: Thank you for being such a great boss. We know it isn't easy being you—with all the pressures and responsibilities that you have. We also know that we're not the easiest bunch to deal with. But with all that you have going on, and with all that we sometimes throw your way, you still manage to remain considerate and understanding. You show us, by your behaviors, that you realize it's challenging for all of us in the workshop too. That makes us appreciate you even more. We really do look forward to your regular visits to the shop floor. We like it when you stop to chat with each of us to see how things are going. It hasn't always been that way, but that doesn't matter. It's that way now, and we're grateful that it is. It's great when you ask us about the problems, challenges, and obstacles that we face in filling our orders and meeting deadlines. You really listen—showing us that our feelings are important—that we are important. We like it when you occasionally work next to us—giving us a hand and keeping you in touch with the operation. But the thing we appreciate the most is when you ask what you can do to make things easier and better for us, and better for the workshop—and then you DO those that are reasonable and appropriate. Thank you, Santa, for making the effort to see things through our eyes…for walking in these smaller, yet none-the-less important shoes. Your feet may not fit in them, but your heart most definitely does. The Elves. (5:40–41)

Organizations require both a chain of command and a chain of understanding. (7:20)

Employee loyalty begins with employer loyalty. Your employees should know that if they do the job they were hired to do with a reasonable amount of competence and efficiency, you will support them. (Harvey Macke, Business Executive, *New York Times* best-selling author and syndicated columnist)

How we treat people is always a choice, and if we choose not to be respectful, it can come back to bite us. (Alison Levine, author of *On the Edge: The Art of High-Impact Leadership*)

It's about communication. It's about honesty. It's about treating people in the organization as deserving to know the facts. You don't try to give them half the story. You don't try to hide the story. You treat them as true equals, and you communicate and you communicate and communicate. (Louis V. Gerstner Jr., former CEO of IBM)

Important components to consider when developing an implementation plan for increasing accessibility to employees, conveying and showing respect, being supportive, developing positive relationships, and consistently doing what is right should include the following: There is no getting around it. I must model the behaviors that I expect from others. I must take the *lead*. I must be the first to "walk the talk" when it comes to things like following *all* our rules and procedures, treating *everyone* with dignity and respect, *always* telling the truth, *never* breaking a promise or commitment, building superior quality in *everything* I do, *continually* giving my best effort, and *consistently* taking a stand for what is right (5:69).

5. To be skillful regarding bringing about change by not pushing events before their time, complimenting individuals regarding their past and present efforts and achievements, introducing new challenges and explaining in detail why change is needed and the potential benefits, allowing for discussion and reflection and even discourse, soliciting ideas for implementation of change and possible alternatives, identifying resources necessary for success, and always remaining patient throughout any change process

    By communicating the critical factors of organizational transformation, leaders can motivate and prepare employees for changes within the organization. If the organization has been performing well, very few people would arguably be interested in changes…that helped them achieve success in the first place. However, many organizations are realizing that success is more closely defined by organizational agility and continuous improvement rather than past achievements. Therefore, one of the most important roles that leaders must play is that of coach and change agent. (2, para:218)

Change is a necessary way of life in most organizations. The term "work change" refers to any alteration that occurs in the work environment. Work change is…complicated by the fact that it does not produce a direct adjustment… Instead, it operates through each employee's attitudes to produce a response that is conditioned by feelings toward the change. Since management initiates much change, it primarily is responsible for implementing change successfully. Management often is called a change agent because its role is to initiate change and help make it work. Though management initiates change, employees typically control its final success. They are the ones who actually make most changes operate. For these reasons, employee support becomes a major goal in the change process. (4, para:198–209)

Because of the costs associated with change, proposals are not always desirable. They require careful analysis to determine usefulness. Unless changes can provide benefits above costs, there is no reason for the changes. In determining benefits and costs, all types of each must be considered. It is useless to examine only economic benefits and costs, because even if there is a net economic benefit, the social or psychological costs may be too large. (4:202–203)

There's an old saying (although it wasn't old when I first heart it…and neither was I) that goes like this: The only constant in life and in business is change. (5:44)

God grant me the serenity to accept things I cannot change, the courage to change the things

I can, and the wisdom to know the difference. (Reinhold Niebuhr, American theologian and public affairs commentator)

Nothing is so painful to the human mind as a great and sudden change. (Mary Shelley, English novelist and essayist)

The entrepreneur always searches for change, responds to it as an opportunity. (Peter Drucker, American management consultant and author)

Important components to consider when developing an implementation plan for planning and implementing change should include the following: (1) understanding the principles of *unfreezing* or casting aside old ideas and practices so that new ones can be learned, then *changing* or introducing new ideas and practices so employees can learn and perform in new ways, and finally *refreezing* or insuring that what has been learned is integrated into actual practice; (2) accepting the typical organizational learning curve that needs to take place so that employees have adequate time to accept and adapt to the change by getting rid of old habits and implementing new habits; (3) building support for change, involving employees through group participation and interaction, and accepting input to foster an understanding regarding the need for change and how to implement the change without disrupting the organization's social system more than necessary; (4) showing capable leadership by providing clear details related to the need for change and demonstrating that the need for change is impersonal; (5) providing actual rewards for employees to elicit their support; (6) assuring employees that their benefits and security will not be affected as the result of change implementation; (7) keeping employees informed throughout the change process with accurate, honest, and ongoing communication; and (8) working with unions, if they exist within your organization, throughout the change

process to elicit and show support for the needed changes since unions function primarily to either support or prevent change in the workplace (4, para:209–215).

6. To spend time teaching and mentoring all employees (i.e., fostering organizational knowledge and experiential learning) regarding the main components necessary for organizational success and adapting to change

Regardless of size and industry, the majority of organizations devote considerable time and resources to developing unique, profitable competencies. Many researchers and organizations look to knowledge to provide this competitive advantage, with the expectation that knowledge can be made to contribute to a firm's performance…"one sure source lasting competitive advantage is knowledge." There is general consensus in the research literature and the popular press that several key factors are needed to implement and embed "organizational learning" into the fabric of an organization: 1) the influence of leadership on individual and organizational culture; 2) creating a culture conducive to organizational learning; 3) improving the quality of knowledge and individual acquires, while facilitating the sharing of that knowledge with others in the organization; 4) generating new, actionable knowledge as a result of knowledge shared or transferred within the organization; and 5) developing a competitive advantage with the newly, generated knowledge… (2, para:9–10)

In the 1950s and 1960s a new, integrated type of training originated known as organization development (OD). Organizational development is an intervention strategy that uses group processes to focus on the whole culture of an organization in order to bring about planned change. It seeks to change beliefs, attitudes, values, structures, and practices so that an organization can better adapt to technology and live with the fast pace of change. OD arose in response to needs. Conventional training methods often had limited success for building better organizational behavior, so a new approach was needed. (4, para:221)

Our nation cannot prevail as the dominant world power if its Leadership is contained in one man. Even I, Attila, cannot accomplish for you what you are not willing to accomplish for yourselves. (10–73)

Sometimes, the experts forget they were once beginners. You must be gentle with beginners; they have great potential to be experts. (Lilly Gifty Akita, founder of Smart Youth Volunteers)

Leaders...should influence others...in such a way that it builds people up, encourages and edifies them so they can duplicate this attitude in others. (Bob Goshen, leadership author and leader development consultant)

An organization's ability to learn, and translate learning into action rapidly, is the ultimate competitive advantage. (Jack Welch, former CEO of General Electric)

Important components to consider when developing an implementation plan for teaching and mentoring all employees regarding gaining organizational knowledge and experiential

learning related to the main components necessary for organizational success and adapting to change should include the following: (1) Develop a comprehensive plan that focuses on the whole organization so it can respond more effectively to learning and change at all levels. (2) Use a systems orientation that focuses on how all parts of the organization affect each other, including structures, processes, attitudes, and personnel relationships. (3) Consider utilizing a skilled change agent to lead who understands the value of employee education and who may be either an expert from within the organization or an outside consultant. (4) Utilize a problem-solving approach that focuses on real, interesting, and stimulating organizational issues. (5) Implement, when appropriate, actual experiential learning for employees so they encounter actual real-life organizational environmental situations that can be reflected upon and assimilated into ongoing practices. (6) Utilize processes, such as group discussions and intergroup projects, to open up communication, build trust, encourage responsiveness, and improve interpersonal relations. (7) Encourage and accept honest feedback so that employees learn to participate in effective decision-making and also learn how to take self-correcting actions on their own. (8) Have ready contingency options to allow for training and learning flexibility since there usually is more than one right way to experience problem-solving and goal attainment. (9) Utilize a total teamwork approach and process throughout the organization, emphasizing both small and large group team experiences (4, para:221–224).

7. To see that employees are treated fairly, appreciated for the positive difference they make with recognition for their contributions with the use of positive rather than negative reinforcement whenever possible, and to work within an organizational environment climate that they can be comfortable in and proud of

In a recent study collecting data from over four million workers throughout the world, three primary categories were identified as what workers want most from their organization: 1) Equity— to be treated justly, with respect, in a safe workplace with a reasonable workload, satisfactory pay, and fringe benefits; 2) Achievement—to take pride in one's accomplishments, be recognized for one's achievements, and to work for an organization which one can be proud of; and 3) Camaraderie—to have warm, interesting and cooperative relationships with others, teamwork, a sense of community, and friendliness. (2, para:14)

Behavior primarily is encouraged through positive reinforcement. Positive reinforcement provides a favorable consequence that encourages repetition of a behavior. (4:71)

Dear Santa: This year I only want one thing—a manager who cares as much about me as the work I'm doing. It's hard to be committed when there's no reciprocation. Please help! (5:14)

Leaders should influence others in such a way that it builds people up, encourages and edifies them so they can duplicate this attitude in others. (Robert Goshen, managing director of Ameriprise Financial)

If you fail to honor your people, they will fail to honor you. It is said of a good leader that when the work is done, the aim is fulfilled. The people will say, "We did it ourselves." (Lao Tzu, Ancient Chinese philosopher and writer)

When a manager recognizes an employee's behavior, personally and sincerely, both feel proud, gratified, and happy. There's a human connection that transcends the immediate culture to create a shared bond. This power is stronger than you might think; indeed, it's power that holds together great organizational cultures. (Erik Mosley and Derek Irvine, coauthors of *The Power of Thanks: How Social Recognition Empowers Employees and Creates a Best Place to Work*)

Important components to consider when developing an implementation plan for fair employee treatment, appreciation and recognition for their contributions with the use of positive rather than negative reinforcement whenever possible, all within an organizational environment that they can be comfortable in and proud of, should include the following: (1) Create an environment that develops trust with employees supported by equitable workload assignments. (2) Create jobs that provide employees with a useful feeling and reasonable job pressures. (3) Create jobs that develop the opportunity to advance based on successful performance and a willingness to take on more responsibility. (4) Notice employee achievements with regular recognition and tangible rewards. (5) Allow for employee participation in decision-making that related to their job responsibilities and also to the overall improvement of the organization. (6) Make certain that organizational bureaucracy, structures, and controls are fair to all employees and are applied consistently throughout the organization (Richard A. Pazasis, Retired Executive and Author of *Guide to Becoming an Effective Manager: Thoughts for Consideration*).

8. To develop, over time, a win-win and healthy partnership-type organizational climate that advocates for moving toward a more "flat-type" span of managerial organizational structure with a more participative win-win

managerial decision-making process, and also focusing on employee personal health and happiness, even within large organizations

All too often bureaucracy—rules and procedures—get in the way of getting the job done efficiently and well. In the partnership organizational model, people at all levels work together for common goals. The partnership organization embodies win-win, basic trust, a long-term perspective, high performance standards, confidence in workers competence, joint decision making, open communication, mutual influence, mutual assistance, recognition, respectful day-to-day treatment, and sharing of financial gains. (2, para:15)

Win/Win is a frame of mind and heart that constantly seeks mutual benefit in all human interactions. Win/Win means that agreements or solutions are mutually beneficial, mutually satisfying. With a Win/Win solution, all parties feel good about the decision and feel committed to the action plan. Win/Win sees life as a cooperative, not a competitive arena. Most people tend to think in terms of dichotomies; strong or weak, hardball or softball, win or lose. But that kind of thinking is fundamentally flawed. It's based on power and position rather than on principle. Win/Win is based on the paradigm that there is plenty for everyone, that one person's success is not achieved at the expense or exclusion of the success of others. (3, para:207)

A basic idea of a classical organization is the span of management (or span of supervision), which refers to the number of people a manager directly manages. Many factors determine the number of employees that one person can manage effectively. Some of these are capacity and skill of the manager, complexity of the worked supervised, capacity and skill of the employees managed, stability of operations, contacts with other chains of command, contacts outside the organization, and geographic distance of subordinates. A small span in an organization causes a tall structure and a large span causes a flat structure. Each structure has its advantages and limitations. In the tall structure, closer coordination and control are permitted because each manager works with fewer people, so there tends to be less conflict and ambiguity. However, communication lines are longer, providing more opportunities for misinterpretation editing. The flat structure has a shorter, simpler communication chain, but managers have so many people to direct that they cannot spend much time face-to-face with any one member or group. In the tall organization, employees tend to be more "boss-oriented." Since their superior is interacting with them regularly day by day, the employees tend to spend much time trying to please their superior. Since the flat structure is more free of hierarchical controls, employees tend to prefer it. One study reported those in flat organizations have greater job satisfaction, less stress, and better production than those in tall organizations. (4, para:249–251)

Probably the most important by-product of meetings is that people who participate in making a decision feel more strongly motivated to accept it and carry it out. In many instances this is more than a by-product—it is the primary purpose of the meeting. Meetings undoubtedly are one of the best means available to commit people to carry out a course of action. A person who has helped make a decision is more interested in seeing it work. Furthermore, if several group members are involved in carrying out a decision, group discussion helps each understand the part others will play, so they can coordinate their efforts. (4:187)

Important components to consider when developing an implementation plan for a win-win and healthy partnership-type organizational climate, with a "flat-type" organizational structure and a more participative managerial process should include the following: (1) When structuring or restructuring the organization, create an organizational chart that begins to reduce the distance between workers and leaders (or managers). (2) Design job descriptions that increase each workers autonomy and influence on decision-making. (3) Build jobs so that they include upward mobile career paths for successful workers. (4) Minimize outsourcing of jobs whenever possible. (5) Place all workers on salary if possible. (6) Provide various types of training programs so that all workers have the opportunity to grow and be successful. (7) Offer profit sharing/stock ownership to all workers. (8) Encourage workers to take care of their personal health (e.g., diet, exercise, healthy lifestyles, stress reduction), and encourage and support them in their lives outside of work (i.e., develop a balance between work and family). (9) Expect supervisors to be more supportive of workers and to recognize and reward workers for excellent performance and provide average and below-average workers with resources to meet organizational performance standards. (10) Create a sense of community both inside and outside the organization through participation, involvement, and philanthropy (2, para:20–21).

Important components to consider when developing an implementation plan for successful decision-making should include the following: General Processes: (1) Remembering the mission of your organization; (2) taking enough time to gather all the facts; (3) gathering employee input from all levels of the organization; (4) determining both the financial and human results (i.e., costs) of your decision on the entire organization; (5) having a specific implementation plan for change with the necessary resources for success available; and (6) and not allowing influence from those not knowledgeable about the organization to determine your decision. Specific Processes: (1) Employees should be consulted before making high-impact decisions using any of these three types of methodologies: brainstorming where a group meets face-to-face and openly identifies the problem, then presents all facts related to the problem, followed by the identification of possible solutions for consideration; nominal groups where a group meets face-to-face, but participants are requested to develop solutions independently, followed by group discussion, and finally the submittal of individual solutions by secret ballot, which are presented and discussed; and the Delphi method where, instead of a meeting, all communication regarding the identification of the problem and all recommended solutions are presented individually in writing. (2) When implementing both brainstorming and nominal groups, be sure to first, clearly define the problem; second, request all facts, ideas, and opinions; third, provide facts, ideas, and opinions not presented; fourth, clarify confusions and give examples when appropriate; and fifth, summarize the entire discussions and determine if any agreement has been reached. (3) During meetings be prepared to support all contributions through recognition, reduce any tension and reconcile any disagreements, be prepared to modify any preconceived results you came with, carefully facilitate the participation of all members present, and finally evaluate the group's effectiveness after the meeting's conclusion (4, para:184–188).

9. To accept the position of leadership with the responsibility and willingness to create a positive organizational culture through shared values

Organizational culture is described as a set of shared beliefs and tactic assumptions that establish individual and group perceptions, thoughts, feelings and behaviors…define organizational culture as a "set of shared values," often taken for granted, that help people in an organization understand which actions are considered acceptable and which are considered unacceptable. (2, para:216)

You see. I'm the leader here. And obviously, I have strong influence on the thoughts and behaviors of the elves and reindeer. They rightfully assume that it's okay to do whatever I do. Regardless of what's said or written elsewhere in the workshop, my actions—whether good or bad—are the performance standards that they will follow. (5:69)

It has been my observation over the years that nations, tribes and lesser bands rise and fall on the strength of their leaders and on the ability with which their leaders carry out their responsibilities of office—seeking first the good of the people. (10:60–61)

The quality of a leader is reflected in the standards they set for themselves. (Ray Kroc, former CEO of McDonald's Corporation)

As a leader, I am tough on myself and I raise the standard for everybody; however, I am very caring because I want people to excel at what they are doing so that they can aspire to be me in the future. (Indra Nooyi, former CEO of PepsiCo)

You can only lead others where you yourself [by example] are willing to go. (Lachlan McLean, nationally recognized radio host at ESPN)

Important components to consider when developing an implementation plan for a leadership style that exhibits and creates a positive organizational culture through shared values should include the following: (1) Always displaying your seriousness for the position, (2) living by the golden rule of leadership that is to lead by example, (3) following all the organizational rules and procedures that you expect all employees to follow, (4) always treating everyone with dignity and respect, (5) always telling the truth, (6) never breaking a commitment or promise, (7) pursuing high standards and quality at all times, (8) always giving your best effort to make your organization successful, and (9) by continually taking a stand for what is right (5, para:69).

10. To be courageous when doing your job and making decisions by always doing what is right and what is ethical

A significant concern about organizational behavior is that its knowledge and techniques can be used to manipulate people as well as to help them develop their potential. People who lack respect for the basic dignity of the human being could learn organizational behavior ideas and use them for selfish ends. They could use what they know about motivation or communication to manipulate people without regard for human welfare. People who lack ethical values could use people in unethical ways. (4:521)

Because ethics is so important to us, I can't rely on my example alone for ensuring that everyone does the right thing. So, I make sure that all staff members are well versed in the laws, rules, and procedures that apply to them. We spend a lot of time discussing—in specific, "how to" terms—what it means to be ethical. (5, para:70)

Management is doing things right; leadership is doing the right things. (Peter Drucker, American business management consultant)

If you believe in unlimited quality and act in all your business dealings with total integrity, the rest will take care of itself. (Frank Perdue, CEO of Perdue Farms)

I'm responsible for this company. I stand behind the results. I know the details, and I think the CEO has to be the moral leader of the company... I think high standards are good, but let's not anybody be confused, it's about performance with integrity. That's what you have to do. (Jeffrey Immelt, CEO of General Electric)

To be careless in making decisions is to naively believe that a single decision impacts nothing more than that single decision, for a single decision can spawn a thousand others that were entirely unnecessary or it can bring peace to a thousand places we never knew existed. (Craig D. Lounsbrough, *Author and Certified Life Coach*)

Important components to consider when developing an implementation plan for doing what is right, ethical, and legal for the organization at all times should include the following:

(1) Be legal by knowing and following the law. (2) Be ethical by conforming to accepted professional norms and standards of conduct. (3) Be in sync with organizational mission, goals, and values when making decisions and taking action. (4) Comply with organizational policies and guidelines as you expect employees to do the same. (5) Be comfortable and guilt-free regarding decision-making and how you treat others. (6) Act similarly to what others in your position would do. (7) Be perfectly okay with someone doing it to me. (8) Emulate what the most ethical person that I know would do (5, para:70).

Organization

To be successful, every organization must have a clear organizational structure that is documented and communicated. At a minimum, the structure should include a chart or diagram of its main components (i.e., divisions of personnel and work functions) and how they are connected, including sets of relationships between employees and their job assignments, to meet the organization's vision, mission, and goals.

> Classical organizational structure is established by functional and scalar divisions of work, and is communicated to participants by means of delegation. (4:259)

Clearly depicting an organization's structure can be a complex task, but here are some thoughts for consideration regarding the development and implementation of a clear organizational structure:

1. To chart out (i.e., in a flowchart or diagram) the organization's structure, which may include, but not be limited to, levels and connections between departments, personnel, job functions, and communication links that tie the main components required to accomplish the organization's vision, mission, and goals

   Most organizations depend upon classical organization for building their structures because it

66

deals with the essential elements in an institution, such as power, responsibility, division of labor, specialization, and interdependence of parts. Organizational structure is significant because it partly determines the power of people in organizations and their perceptions of their roles. It also affects job satisfaction. The organizing process may be perceived in two ways. It may be considered as a process of construction in which a great number of small work units are built into jobs, departments, divisions, and finally a whole institution. Or an organization may be viewed as a process of analysis by which a particular area of work is subdivided into divisions, departments, and finally jobs assigned to particular people. (4, para:243)

Organizational charts are a good way to visualize reporting relationships and team roles in businesses, nonprofit organizations, educational institutions and governments. (smartdraw.com)

The organizational chart is a diagram showing graphically the relation of one to another, or others, of a company. It is also to show the relation of one department to another, or others, or of one function of an organization to another, or others. This chart is valuable in that it enables one to visualize a complete organization, by means of the picture it presents. (Wikipedia)

I was never more disappointed when I arrived at an organization's worksite, to evaluate it as the lead team consultant, to become aware that management did not have and was not able to provide any document showing the formal structure of itself. (Richard A. Pazasis, retired executive and author of *Guide to Becoming an Effective Manager: Thoughts for Consideration*)

Important components to consider when developing an implementation plan for having a documented organizational chart for one's organization should include the following: (1) An understanding of the principles behind the need for an organizational chart. Management Structure: The organizational chart shows the individual roles and chain of command within the business structure. A well-managed company will function according to its framework. An organizational chart is useful as a valuable management tool. It allows managers to effectively manage goals, develop strategy, and improve interaction between individuals and entire departments. Other Organizational Structures: An organization chart can also be used to show other types of hierarchies. A Planning Tool: You can also use an organizational chart for planning purposes and to organize employees into a workforce or work groups. An Employee Reference: Many organizations give a copy of the organization chart to each employee. Once an employee finds their position on the chart, he/she can see immediately who his/her supervisor is, who his/her coworkers are, and how he/she fits into the organization. (2) That there are four basic types of organizational charts. Functional Top-down: A functional, top-down organizational chart reflects a traditional business structure. The structure shows the CEO at the top, followed by other senior management, middle managers, and so on down the line. The structure is usually divided into traditional department based on everyone's functional role in the organization. In such an organizational structure, employees with similar skill sets and specialization are grouped together. Divisional Structure: A divisional organizational chart reflects how a company is organized along a product line or specific geography. A company will use a divisional setup when one division is sufficiently independent from another. Matrix Organizational Chart: A matrix organizational chart reflects a company where employees are divided into teams by projects or product led by a project manager but also reports to a functional manager. It shows a company that operates using cross-functional groups instead of vertical silos. Flat Organizational Chart: A flat organization structure will show few or no levels of management between executives and all other employees. This type of structure empowers self-management and a greater decision-making ability for every employee within his/her group (para:SmartDraw Enterprise, para:smartdraw.com).

2. To make clear each employee's connection and role to the organization with written job descriptions (i.e., position title, qualifications, job responsibilities, salary and benefits, and performance expectations)

Crafting a compelling job description is essential to helping you attract the most qualified candidates for your job. Your job descriptions are where you start marketing your company and your job to future hire. The key to writing effective job descriptions is to find the perfect balance between providing enough detail so candidates understand the role and your company while keeping your description concise. (indeed.com)

A job description...is a document that describes the general tasks, or other related duties, and responsibilities of a position. It may specify the functionary to whom the position reports, specifications such as qualifications or skills needed by the person in the jib, and salary range. (Wikipedia)

A job description is an internal document that clearly states the essential job requirements, job duties, job responsibilities, and skills required

to perform a specific role. A more detailed job
description will cover how success is measured
in the role so it can be used during performance
evaluations. (Jonathan Jasinski, Microplant
Nurseries Inc.)

**Important components to consider when developing an
implementation plan for the development and publication of
employee job descriptions should include the following: (1)
Heading Information: This should include job title, pay grade or
range, reporting relationship (by position, not individual), hours
or shifts, and the likelihood of overtime or weekend work. (2)
Summary Objective of the Job: List the general responsibilities
and descriptions of key tasks and their purposes; relationships
with customers, coworkers, and others; and the results expected
of incumbent employees. (3) Qualifications: State the education,
experience, training, and technical skills necessary for entry into
this job. (4) Special Demands: This should include any extraor-
dinary conditions applicable to the job (e.g., heavy lifting, expo-
sure to temperature extremes, prolonged standing, or travel). (5)
Job Duties and Responsibilities: Only two features of job responsibility are important—identifying tasks that comprise about 90
to 95 percent of the work done and listing tasks in order of time
consumed (or sometimes, in order of importance) (para:Cathleen
Yonahara, Freeland Cooper and Foreman LLP).**

3. To staff (i.e., identify, appoint, and retain) the organization with only qualified employees not only who will be an
   excellent fit within the organization but also who will help
   and not hinder the organization's achievement toward its
   vision, mission, and goals

   Talented people are critical to the success of a
   company, therefore the importance of strengthening the firm's talent pool is now heightened.
   (2:5)

Now I do things much differently… I've come to realize that: 1) Because it's employees who ultimately make our mission happen, staffing is my single most important responsibility; 2) The time I spend hiring the right way is nothing compared to the time I'll have to spend dealing with the wrong reindeer. (5:21)

The secret of my success is that we have gone to exceptional lengths to hire the best people in the world. (Steve Jobs, former CEO of Apple Inc.)

The smartest business decision you can make is to hire qualified people. Bringing the right people on board saves you thousands, and your business will run smoothly and efficiently. (Brian Tracy, self-development author and consultant)

Never hire someone who knows less than you do about what he's hired to do. (Malcolm Forbes, entrepreneur and *Forbes* Magazine publisher)

Important components to consider when developing an implementation plan for the hiring of employees should include the following: (1) Identify hiring need: Identify new or vacated positions to be filled. (2) Plan: Make certain that everyone involved in the hiring process understands and commits to the process and communication channels to be used, including the development of a time line, recruitment plan, criteria for initial candidate screening, who is involved in the selection, interview questions, and the recording of all interviews. (3) Create a job description: The agreed-upon job requirements form the basis for the job description, including, but not limited to, the job title, job qualifications, essential functions of the job, compensation and benefits, perks, and sometimes job expectations. (4) Post and promote job openings: Advertise both within and

without the organization including the use of your organization's website, online job boards, social media, job fairs, and industry publications. (5) Recruiting: If available and if necessary, utilize professional recruiting consultants or online job recruiting firms. (6) Applicant screening: After the creation and publication of the application form, those identified to initially screen applicants should conduct a paper screening as the applications arrive, withdraw unqualified candidates, and inform qualified candidates regarding the next step in the hiring process. (7) Interviews: Some type of in-person interview process should take place where top candidates are questioned regarding their experience, skills, work history, and availability and are rated so that top leadership may consider which candidates deserve a final interview. (8) Applicant talent assessment: In the case of specific technical skill-based or physical suitability-based positions, candidates should be given preemployment written or performance tests. (9) Background/ reference checks: Before making a final offer, background and reference checks should be conducted on the top candidates. (10) Job offer and hiring: Offering the job includes providing an offer letter stating the salary, start date, and other terms and conditions of employment and making certain that the candidate understands and agrees to the terms of employment, followed by the joint signing of an employment agreement. (11) Hiring and onboarding: Once the candidate has been officially hired, all required employment papers should be completed and then the scheduling of a formal plan to welcome in the new employee, prepare the new employee for his/her workspace, and initiate any required training (para:SmartRecruiters.com).

4. To describe in writing (i.e., in a brochure format), publish, and disseminate, both internally and externally, the organization's official mission, goals, rules, procedures, programs, and services

A brochure is an informative paper document...
that can be folded into a template, pamphlet or
leaflet. (Wikipedia)

Important components to consider when developing an implementation plan for developing and making available, for both internal and external distribution, updated brochures with descriptions of the organization's mission, goals, rules, procedures, programs, and services should include (1) a boldface headline that captures your audience's attention and (2) only the very basic information that the organization wishes to communicate in an easy-to-read format that avoids using big words so not to confuse the reader (para: Article on Company Brochures at entrepreneur.com, May 25, 2007).

Goals

A chievable goals, with specific objectives and strategies leading to the implementation of each goal, are the road map to
an organization's success. They need to be related directly to
the organization's vision and mission, they need to be doable with
the appropriation of resources to ensure success, and they need to be
communicated.

> Setting goals is the first step in turning the invis-
> ible into the visible. (Tony Robbins, author and
> entrepreneur)

> Our goals can only be reached through a vehi-
> cle of a plan, in which we must fervently believe,
> and upon which we must vigorously act. There is
> no other route to success. (Pablo Picasso, Spanish
> artist)

The process to develop effective goals, objectives, and strategies
will take a considerable amount of time but is a necessary one. Here
are some thoughts for consideration regarding the development of
organizational goals, objectives, and strategies:

1. To include representation (i.e., participative management)
   from a variety of stakeholders, from both within and without the organization, when developing the organization's
   goals, objectives, and strategies

There is an enormous amount to be gained by involving the workforce in organization improvement. They have much to contribute, especially about improvements in their own jobs and work areas. They are motivated to make work changes that they have initiated. Involvement—treating them as intelligent and dedicated employees—is a sign of respect for them that boosts their morale and commitment. This is true at all organizational levels. (2:49)

Participative managers consult with their followers, bringing them in on...decisions... Participative managers still retain ultimate responsibility...but they have learned to share operating responsibility with those who perform the work. (4,para:152)

Whether they're in direct production and delivery, or a "behind the scenes" support function, everyone has goals—including me. Our goals are very specific yet flexible—allowing for changing conditions and circumstances. And because staff "buy-in" and commitment are so important to achieving our objectives, I make sure that everyone has input in the goal-setting process. (5:28)

Important components to consider when developing an implementation plan for including all stakeholders in the development of an organization's goals, objectives, and strategies should include the following: (1) There must be time to participate before action is required and not in emergency situations. (2) The potential benefits for participation should be greater than its costs so that participants do not ignore their main responsibilities. (3) The subject of participation must be relevant to the stakeholders' environment; otherwise, stakeholders will look

upon it merely as busywork. (4) The participants involved should have the ability, such as intelligence, knowledge, and skill to participate. (5) The participants must be able to mutually communicate—to talk each other's language—in order to exchange ideas. (6) Neither party should feel that its position is threatened by participation and think that their status or position will be adversely affected. (7) Participation for deciding any course of action in an organization can take place only within certain restrictions, such as not violating laws, policies, and collective bargaining agreements (4, para:156–157).

2.   To develop, in an action plan format, goals, objectives, and strategies that can be delivered (i.e., they are doable) and that can be broken down into manageable parts, including *what* needs to be accomplished, *why* it needs to be accomplished, *when* does it need to be accomplished, *who* will be involved in its accomplishment, *how* will it be accomplished, *what* resources will be needed to ensure its accomplishment, and *how* will its progress be measured

Once our individual and group goals are identified, we move into the planning (making "the list") phase. Plans provide us with the direction, focus, and organization we need to stay on task. And since none of us here at the Pole have perfect memories, we make sure that they're written action plans. (5:29)

Goals are the fuel in the furnace of achievement. (Brian Tracy, self-development consultant and author)

A goal is like a strenuous exercise—it makes you stretch. (Mary Kay Ash, business executive and founder of Mary Kay Cosmetics)

Important components to consider when developing an implementation plan for developing an action plan necessary for organizational goal attainment should include the following: (1) What needs to be accomplished? (2) Why does it need to be done and how does it contribute to our overall mission? (3) When does it need to be accomplished? (4) Where am I/are we now in relation to this goal? (5) Who will be involved in accomplishing this? (6) How will it be accomplished? (7) What specific steps and activities are involved, and what resources are required? (5, para:29).

3. To build in benchmark time lines for the ongoing measurement and evaluation of all goals, objectives, and strategies to track progress and to reassess and allow flexibility for appropriate changes as needed to ensure maximum achievement (i.e., to ensure that the goals, objectives, and strategies remain valid and doable in light of changing conditions)

We schedule (as in: set specific times on our calendars) frequent progress checks as part of the work-planning process. I meet with teams and individuals—and they meet among themselves, without me—to measure the status of our goals against predetermined progress benchmarks. (5:31)

Critical to a Hun's success is a clear understanding of what a king wants. A Hun's goals should always be worthy of his efforts. As a nation, we would accomplish more if Huns behaved as though national goals were as important to them as personal goals. Chieftains should always aim high, going after things that will make a difference rather than seeking the safe path of mediocrity. Superficial goals lead to superficial results.

A Hun's performance does not always results in
desired performance. (10:106)

Important components to consider when developing an
implementation plan for measuring, evaluating, and modifying
if needed organizational goals should include the following: (1)
Ask if each goal is still valid and doable. (2) Ask where we should
be in terms of attaining each goal. (3) Ask if any conditions or
circumstances have changed since we originally set each goal.
(4) Ask if we need to make any changes to our goals, our action
plans, or our performance levels (5, para:31).

Communication

Organizations will not be successful without effective communication. Communication is the glue that keeps all of the main components of the organization together. When the glue remains strong and intact, all components remain firmly bonded, and the organization withstands erosion. But when the glue erodes, the organization weakens until the glue is replaced with new glue.

> Workers' frustrations with an absence of adequate communication are among the most negative findings of employee surveys. (2:53)

For communication to be effective, it must be two-way (i.e., sending as well as receiving information). Here are some thoughts for consideration regarding making certain that an organization's communication processes are and remain effective:

1. To communicate with each other as managers to ensure consistent communication throughout the organization

    > Meetings among management should conclude with a specific plan for communicating the results of meetings to employees. (2:53)

    > Sometimes there is a tendency to say "Let's improve employee communication; manage-

ment can take care of itself." The result is that the entire communication effort is directed toward employees, but there are a number of reasons why management communication deserves equal emphasis. (4:419)

Important components to consider when developing an implementation plan for improved communication between managers should include the following: (1) the scheduling of regular meetings for managers to prevent isolation, share information received from upward communication, discuss both successes and issues, recommend solutions to problems, and develop downward communication to employees and (2) making employees aware of the scheduled meetings among managers and sharing with them the results of these meetings, especially concerning any actions to be taken that would affect employees (4,para:419).

2. To make certain that all types of communication disseminated throughout the organization, both written and verbal, are clear and are understood by the expected recipients

Communication is the transfer of information and understanding from one person to another person. It is a way of reaching others with ideas, facts, thoughts, and values. It is a bridge of meaning among people so that they can share what they feel and know. By using this bridge, a person can cross safely the river of misunderstanding that sometimes separates people. (4:399)

I know you believe you understand what you think I said, but you may not be aware that what you heard is not what he meant. (7:54)

Important components to consider when developing an implementation plan for an improved communication process

should include the following: Step 1. Develop an idea or thought that the sender wishes to transmit. This is a key step because unless there is a worthwhile message, all the other steps are somewhat useless. Step 2. Encode the idea into suitable words, charts, or other symbols for transmission. At this point, the sender determines the method of transmission so that the words and symbols may be organized in suitable fashion for the type of transmission. Step 3. When the message finally is developed, transmit it by the method chosen. Senders also choose certain channels, and they communicate with careful timing. Senders also try to keep their communication channel free of barriers or interference so that messages have a chance to reach receivers and hold their attention. Step 4. Transmission allows another person to receive a message. In this step, initiative transfers to receivers who tune to receive the message. If it is oral, they need to be good listeners. If the receiver does not function, the message is lost. Step 5. Decode the message so that it can be understood. The sender wants the receiver to understand the message exactly as it was sent. Although some receivers may be uncooperative and may try to misunderstand, normally they make a genuine attempt to understand the intended message. Even with the best intentions, a receiver may not understand exactly what the sender intended because the perceptions of the two people are different. Understanding can occur only in a receiver's mind. A communicator may make others listen, but there is no way to make others understand. The receiver alone chooses whether to understand or not. Step 6. Utilization of the communication by the receiver. The receiver may ignore it, perform the task assigned, store the information provided, or do something else. Senders always need to communicate with care. And then there is the "Rule of Five" to ensure effective communication. Receivers need to receive, understand, accept, use, and give feedback. If used properly, its use provides a better understanding for both parties. Also, the sender should be aware of the following that can interfere with communication: *personal barriers* or communication interference that arise from human emotions, values, poor listening habits; *physical barriers* or communication interference that occur in the environment in which the communication takes place (e.g., noise, distance between people, wall, and static interference); *semantics barriers* or the science of meaning. Nearly all communication is symbolic. The meaning that receivers take depends on their attitudes, experiences, and listening skills, including an understanding of the words and symbols being used within the communication (e.g., readability, multiple meanings, context) and body language interpretation related to oral in-person communication, and listening skills (4, para:400–413).

3. To develop various procedures to listen to employees and clients and include them in assessing the implementation of the organization's vision, mission, goals, objectives, and strategies and leadership effectiveness and to seek and use feedback from employees and clients through managerial visibility and other means (e.g., walking around, meetings, surveys, telephone calls, e-mails, open office, advisory groups)

    Most managers must discipline themselves to communicate regularly because it's not a natural instinct for them. Schedule regular employee meetings that have no purpose other than two-way communication. (2:53)

    So, I began doing employee attitude surveys and conducting focus groups. I even established a "North Pole feedback hot line" to help find out what everyone thought about me as a leader, and to provide a vehicle for collecting input on how I could improve. (5:38)

    Certain characteristics of feedback should prevail. It should be nonjudgmental, positive, reciprocal, useful, timely, and objective. (7:25)

Perhaps listening is the least developed, yet most needed management skill. (7:71)

Most of the successful people I've known are the ones who do more listening than talking. (Bernard Baruch, former American financier and investor)

One of the most sincere forms of respect is actually listening to what another has to say. (Bryant H. McGill, entrepreneur and author)

You have to be willing sometimes to listen to some remarkable bad opinions. Because if you say to someone, "That's the silliest thing I've ever heard; get on out of here!"—then you'll never get anything out of that person again, and you might as well have a puppet on a string or a robot. (John Bryan, former CEO of Sara Lee Corporation)

Important components to consider when developing an implementation plan for improved upward communication with employees should include the following: (1) making certain that two-way communication takes place on a regular basis both between the organization and its external environment and internally with all employees; (2) developing written surveys for periodic use, with both clients and employees, to collect valuable input regarding how the organization and its leadership are performing; (3) making personal contact with clients and employees, both individually and in small groups, to elicit oral feedback on how the organization and its leadership are performing; (4) implementing anonymous hotlines and suggestion boxes to collect additional feedback; (5) accepting all feedback and be willing to act on the feedback in a timely manner; and 6) publishing the results of all surveys and what action will or has been taken by leadership (5, para:38–41).

4.   To walk in the employees' shoes from time to time by going into the trenches of your organization to experience various employee roles

> We have all heard the quote, "Before you judge a person, walk a mile in their shoes." This saying acts as a reminder to practice empathy. But what is at the core of empathy, and why is it so crucial in the workplace? Empathy is "the ability to understand and share the feelings of another." Research has shown over and over again that empathy is a critical element for leaders… It should come as no surprise then that empathy is the cornerstone of a leader's effectiveness in keeping stakeholders confident, employees engaged, and customers loyal. (Tony Gambill, leadership and talent development consultant of CREO Inc.)

Important components to consider when developing an implementation plan for managing by "walking around" should include the following: (1) Develop your understanding regarding human motivation that includes an employee's need to control one's own behavior and goals, feel a sense of belonging and security in relationships, and master the challenging tasks assigned. (2) Increase your empathy for employees by asking yourself: What do I know about each employee, including about his personal background, current life situation, and employment position within the organization? What questions will I ask each employee when I walk around my organization? What will I learn from each employee by being a good listener? (3) Ask the following questions when walking around: How do you feel about your current work situation? What can I do to improve your work situation? How do you feel about working with management and your employee colleagues? Does our organization support you for success and advancement, and if not, how can we improve

your work situation in this regard? (Tony Gambill, leadership and talent development consultant, CREO Inc.).

5. To always follow up as quickly as possible regarding responses to questions, concerns, and suggestions

   A straightforward communications approach is best. Many employees are quite skeptical about management's motives and can quickly see through "spin." Tell it like it is. (2:53)

   When upward communication is received, management needs to respond to it in order to encourage further upward messages. Conversely, lack of response suppresses upward communication... (4:428)

Important components to consider when developing an implementation plan for an improved communication approach with employees related to receiving and making timely responses should include the following: Encouraging employee upward communication regarding any matters that may happen when a supervisor could be held accountable by those at higher levels, when there is a disagreement or an issue likely to cause controversy within or between units of the organization, and when advice is required from the supervisor or coordinator involving recommendations for changes in policy and procedure and that will enable higher management to improve performance (4, para:428).

6. To implement periodic formal communication audits of the organization, publish the results, and make necessary improvements as recommended within the audit's findings and recommendations.

A well conceived communication audit, or communications effectiveness study, is an effective management tool that helps target messages, media and audiences and improves the effectiveness of communication efforts. (Peter Hollister and Patricia Trubow, author of "Your Organization is Ready for a Communication Effectiveness Study," Public Relations Tactics, July 2005)

Communications research programs often start with a communication audit, a method of research that determines how your core audiences perceive your organization. (Rebecca Hart, author of "Measuring Success: How to Sell Communications Audits to Internal Audiences," Public Relations Tactics, April 2006)

Important components to consider when developing an implementation plan for implementing periodic communication audits within an organization should include the following: (1) Develop a simple series of standard questions, in a written questionnaire format, such as the following: What does your organization look like? What should it look like? Do you know who to report to and is he/she the right person or resource? Are you a resource to a fellow manager or employee and should you be? Do you know communication is reported both downward and upward and is it adequate? Does management call periodic meetings between managers and between employees to communicate and seek input to solve problems, and are these meetings effective? How would you improve communication by strengthening communication gaps in your organization? (2) Distribute the questionnaire to both employees and management. (3) Collect, tabulate, and analyze questionnaire results. (4) Set up one-on-one and group face-to-face interviews, separately, with both managers and employees, to verify and clarify questionnaire

results and to gain additional information. (5) Put all results in a written communication audit report with recommendations for improvements. (6) Publish and distribute communication audit results within the organization. (7) Schedule meetings first with management and then with employees to discuss the results of the communication audit and to seek input regarding how to best implement improvements. (8) Take immediate action to make improvements. (Richard A. Pazasis, retired executive and author of *Guide to Becoming an Effective Manager: Thoughts for Consideration*)

Administration

Administrative procedures, processes, and actions must be efficient to ensure the most cost-effective operations related to all aspects of an organization, including that of management and employee interactions. Achieving the organization's vision, mission, goals, objectives, and strategies should include obtaining, providing, and getting the most out of all valuable resources. Especially during times when resources are limited and increasingly more costly to obtain, the organization's administrative processes must be extremely cognizant of its ability to provide the necessary financial support for the organization to be effective in the most prudent manner possible. In addition, the organization is required to ensure that all proper fiduciary responsibilities, such as legal and financial requirements and procedures, are complied with and to clearly keep records of and communicate such procedures as required. And to do all this, management must utilize effective time management skills!

> Most organizations in the past, whether they were business or government, made their decisions on the basis of economic and technical values. The new emphasis on social responsiveness has led to a socioeconomic model of decision making in which social costs and benefits are considered along with the traditional economic and technical values in decision making. (4:31)

There are other costs in addition to pay. Equipment and floor space may need to be redesigned. In some instances more space and tools will be needed so that teams can work independently. Even work-in-process inventory may have been increased so that individual workers or teams can have enough supplies. In addition, there are substantial training costs in order to prepare employees for their new patterns of work. There also are likely to be temporary quality and output problems during the period of change because existing teamwork among employees is disrupted. Some employees even resign. Although these costs may be acceptable in relation to benefits, they need to be considered carefully. (4:298)

Here are some thoughts for consideration regarding administrative processes that lead to the effective management of organizations:

1. To make the most of time as a leader and manager (i.e., every minute that goes by is lost and cannot be recovered), which should include, but not be limited to, prioritizing managerial tasks on a daily and weekly basis, preparing in advance for meetings and seeing that participants in meetings have preliminary information concerning the content of each meeting, keeping meetings on time and on task and allow for a two-way communication, only scheduling meetings with agenda topics that cannot be communicated via various nonmeeting processes, utilizing time-saving technology for communication and record keeping, and developing/communicating/implementing effective time management processes throughout the organization

    The idea of "time management" may be the biggest misconception of all. For time cannot be managed. At least not in the way other resources can. Business is concerned with the wise management of five kinds of resources: capital, physical, human, information, and time. All of the first four can be manipulated in many directions. But time, the invisible resource is unique, because it is finite. There is only so much of it, and no matter what you do, you can't get more. (6, para:11–12)

Don't be fooled by the calendar. There are only as many days in the year as you make use of. One man gets only a week's value out of a year while another man gets a full year's value out of a week. (Charles Richards, founder of American Society of Mechanical Engineers)

Once you have masters time, you will understand how true it is that most people overestimate what they can accomplish in a year—and underestimate what they can achieve in a decade. (Anthony Robbins, entrepreneur and life coach)

Important components to consider when developing an implementation plan for the improvement of one's own time management (i.e., the manager's personal time management skills) should include the following: (1) Become self-aware of the need to improve your time management skills—sine qua non (i.e., a necessary condition without something is not possible). (2) Plan each day in advance by writing down your schedule, goals, and tasks. (3) Use high-energy hours for most challenging tasks. (4) Create and utilize time more efficiently by addressing gaps in your day for taking on secondary tasks. (5) Defeat any impulse to procrastinate. (6) Reduce clutter using efficient systems for the filing and retrieval of information and documents. (7) Delegate secondary tasks whenever possible. (8) Plan and implement meetings efficiently. (9) Experiment with time man-

agement techniques, and select those that ultimately work best (9, para:first page insert).

2. To make the most of employees by involving them in periodic meetings, when appropriate and possible; to solicit input and recommendations regarding the development and implementation of cost-effective organizational policies, processes, and decisions; and to increase employee motivation to improve their own efficiency

There is an enormous amount to be gained by involving the workforce in organization improvement. They have much to contribute, especially about improvements in their own jobs and work areas. They are motivated to make work the changes that they have initiated. Involvement—treating them as intelligent and dedicated employees—is a sign of respect for them that boosts their morale and commitment. This is true at all organizational level. (2:49)

Meetings are convened for many purposes, such as information, advice, decision making…creative thinking. (4:184)

Because resources are so important to us, we've gone beyond merely relying on goal action plans to insure efficiency. The best example of this is a workshop-wide team we created called "Waste Watcher"… The sole purpose of this group is to identify and eliminate inefficient/Wasteful business practices. (5:32)

The efficiency of most workers is beyond the control of management and depends more than has been supposed upon the willingness of men to do their best. (Sumner Slichter, professor of economics, Harvard University)

Important components to consider when developing an implementation plan for the effective and efficient implementation of meetings to solicit employee input should include the following: (1) Distribute the agenda in advance. (2) Clarify the main objective of the meeting on the agenda. (3) Circulate background material in advance of the meeting. (4) Stay on focus while encouraging the expression of all viewpoints related to the topic. (5) Separate the generation of ideas from evaluating them. (6) Control irrelevant discussions and digressions from the main objective. (7) Rotate record-keeping among group members if a recording secretary cannot be provided. (8) Always end on a positive note. (9) Develop a summary communication document related to the content of the meeting to be distributed throughout the organization. (10) Make a management decision regarding action to be taken as the result of the meeting, and then schedule a meeting with management and employees together to present management's decision and action plan. (11) Evaluate the entire meeting process for future improvements (4, para:190).

3. To ensure that proper fiduciary responsibilities, regarding following procedures and keeping accurate and required records related to all legal and financial requirements, are complied with and to keep on file such records related to such responsibilities and procedures and make such records available upon request or when required to file with the appropriate agencies

A duty dodged is like a debt unpaid; it is only deferred, and we must come back and settle the account at last. (Joseph Fort Newton, author and minister)

> My biggest problem with modernity may lie in
> the growing separation of the ethical and legal.
> (Nassim Nicholas Taleb, risk analyst and author)

Important components to consider when developing an implementation plan for ensuring that proper fiduciary responsibilities and procedures, such as legal and financial requirements, are complied with and to clearly keep records of and communicate such procedures as required should include the following: (1) Before starting up a new organization or moving into the top management position of an existing organization, it is necessary to review and develop a report on its current legal and financial status for compliance and protection. (2) If a medium- to large-size organization, consider either hiring in-house legal counsel and in-house accounting personnel to supervise and manage all legal and financial responsibilities or contract out to a major legal firm and accounting firm to perform such requirements. (3) If a start-up or small-size organization, management should consider either contracting, on a need-to-need basis, with a local qualified attorney and accountant for services, or search the internet for reputable companies that offer low-cost/full-service legal and accounting services, often through providing cost-effective advice and software, including billing/income/payment services, inventory management, federal and state income tax filing, and payroll services, to perform such requirements.

4. To implement discount/bulk/cooperative purchasing practices, the soliciting of price quotes (i.e., bids) from reliable sources, the incorporation of a paper reduction and recycling program, and the reduction of postage and shipping costs, whenever possible

> There are two ways to save money. First, you
> could increase your sales and revenue. Second,
> you could reduce your expenses. (Jonathan Long,
> founder of Uber Brands)

Reducing and reusing take nothing more than a rethink on the way to the shop, and using our imagination with things that we might once have considered junk. (Sheherazade Goldsmith, British environmentalist and author)

Important components to consider when developing an implementation plan for researching and implementing programs to reduce costs by bidding for products and services, recycling, and researching postage and shipping costs should include the following: Regarding bidding, (1) always shop around when looking to purchase products and services and request at least three quotes (i.e., bids) before making a decision, and (2) if local-, state-, or federal-controlled bid lists are available, usually offered to government agencies, take advantage of pre-authorized bid acceptances for products and services you desire, which are usually lower in costs due to bulk bidding and purchasing arrangements. Concerning recycling, (1) start a recycling program to save money since, in the average workplace, about 80 to 90 percent of solid waste is actually recyclable, (2) survey your workplace and figuring out exactly what's going into the trash, (3) identify which products are recyclable, (4) contact your local municipal waste management program or a commercial recycling vendor for the best price, (5) develop an organizational recycling program that is placed in writing and distributed throughout the organization, (6) hold meetings to explain the program and elicit cooperation, (7) appoint a recycling coordinator to supervise the program, (8) offer training to personnel, (9) arrange for pickup and disposal, and (10) evaluate the program for improvements as needed. Regarding postage and shipping, research postal and shipping costs (i.e., usually USPS rates are best if no more than 2 lbs., and the implementation of using USPS postal meters can also reduce costs, but FedEx and UPS are less costly if over 2 lbs. to reduce costs (Richard A. Pazasis, Retired Executive and Author of *Guide to Becoming an Effective Manager: Thoughts for Consideration*).

5. To take advantage of all local, state, and federal incentives to start up or relocate and operate

So, why then do entrepreneurs choose to relocate their business? Reasons include: Potential increase in revenue, Better pool of Employees, Tax breaks, and lower overall cost in doing business. (para:BusinessVibes, December 26, 2015)

Important components to consider when developing an implementation plan for researching local, state, and federal incentives to start up, relocate, or operate a business should include the following: (1) Look for available governmental and private grants to start a business through an internet search. (2) Consider moving to states offering tax incentives for business start-ups and relocations through an internet search. (3) Identify and work with companies that help business relocate through an internet search (Richard A. Pazasis, Retired Executive and Author of *Guide to Becoming an Effective Manager: Thoughts for Consideration*)

6. To utilize technology whenever possible for communication, production, publishing, and record keeping, with a dual backup data and record-keeping storage system at an alternate site to protect all valuable data and records (e.g., backup disks, cloud technology), which will allow management to spend more time on higher-impact responsibilities

Society has discovered that it needs to give more attention to the relationship of technology... As technology changes, jobs also change. Technology tends to require more professional, scientific, and other white-collar workers to keep the system in operating condition. In most advanced installations the ratio of white-collar to blue-collar employees has increased. It seems appropriate to replace routine jobs with machine systems that can do the job faster and better, thus releasing people to do more advanced work... (4, para:263–265)

Important components to consider when developing an implementation plan for the effective use of technology should include the following: (1) Determine all areas where technology can better serve the organization regarding cost-effectiveness. (2) Identify the type of technology equipment, software, and network systems required, and prepare and request at least three bids for consideration from reputable vendors. (3) Select the most cost-effective bids in each area after conducting background checks, with attention to both initial and extended warranties and service maintenance contracts. (4) Appoint or hire at least one individual to supervise an in-house technology department to oversee the installation of the new technology and the scheduling of employee training. (5) Work with vendors to schedule installation, setup, and employee training. (6) Periodically evaluate the technology and any future need for updating and replacement (Richard A. Pazasis, Retired Executive and Author of *Guide to Becoming an Effective Manager: Thoughts for Consideration*).

7. To utilize facilities, materials, and equipment efficiently and effectively, institute a preventive maintenance program for facilities and equipment, implement a periodic equipment replacement program, and provide needed services and supplies for indoor and outdoor facility cleanliness and general upkeep

The future of the workspace is changing, quickly. It's important that facilities managers to stay open to new ideas and concepts that present themselves (Tiffany Rivers, facilities consultant and author)

Your location's cleanliness and sanitation may be one of the most important factors in attracting new customer—and in keeping the ones you've already got. (*QSR Magazine*, April 2010)

Important components to consider when developing an implementation plan for the effective and efficient utilization of facilities/materials/equipment, institution of a preventive maintenance program for facilities and equipment, scheduling of a periodic equipment replacement program, and providing needed cleaning and upkeep services and supplies for both indoor and outdoor facilities should include the following: (1) Utilize the organization's upward communication channels to continually request input, from lower-level management and all other employees, on how best to improve the effectiveness and efficiency concerning facility/material/equipment utilization, facility and equipment maintenance, equipment replacement, and both indoor and outdoor facility cleanliness and upkeep. (2) Require management to develop and implement plans to provide additional resources and training programs to follow up on employee recommendations for improvement. (3) Develop and implement plans for preventative facility and equipment maintenance and for the general cleaning and upkeep of indoor and outdoor facilities, by either hiring in-house specialists or contracting out to commercial providers. (4) Provide in-house facility cleaning and ground's maintenance employees and supplies for both indoor and outdoor facility cleanliness and upkeep or by contracting out to commercial providers (Richard A. Pazasis, Retired Executive and Author of *Guide to Becoming an Effective Manager: Thoughts for Consideration*).

8. To implement cross-training of employees to ensure that there are at least two employees who can perform the same job in case an employee is either temporarily or permanently unable to perform his or her job responsibilities and to develop, among all employees, an appreciation and

understanding concerning how all workers are interdependent in achieving the organization's mission

A series of…successful initiatives include: cross-training and rotating assignments within departments so everyone can understand and appreciate the functions of, and challenges faced by, their co-workers, and a departmental "swap" program that allows individuals to experience how other business units operate…and how we are all interdependent in achieving our overall mission. (5, para:49)

Important components to consider when developing an implementation plan for the cross-training of employees should include the following: (1) Whenever possible, but usually more achievable in a "flat" organization where employees are grouped in teams rather than in a "tall" organization where specializations are spread out in distant work assignments, management should consider offering cross-training options (i.e., when one employee learns another employee's job to fill in or pick up the slack). (2) Such programs should allow for flexibility and other benefits for employees who are assigned or who volunteer for cross-training responsibilities. (3) Benefits should include allowing a colleague to fill in for another when they are out providing the absentee colleague will reciprocate or allow the colleague who fills in to earn future paid time off when requested. (4) Develop and implement voluntary cross-training programs where employees are trained during work hours for full pay or who are offered additional pay to attend cross-training programs during nonwork hour (Richard A. Pazasis, retired executive and author of *Guide to Becoming an Effective Manager: Thoughts for Consideration*).

Management

Coordinated oversight and evaluation is a very important component of effective management and must include monitoring the entire organization on a regular basis (i.e., knowing what is going on at all levels), establishing and implementing personnel evaluation programs for performance accountability, and measuring and evaluating goal attainment by the organization.

> For me, building accountability...involves the following: Keeping my eyes and ears open to what's happening through visits, feedback, reports, meetings, etc., I make sure that I'm aware of what is being done and how it is being accomplished; Providing ongoing feedback. I regularly meet with the elves and reindeer to discuss their performance, share my observations, and reemphasize the importance of integrity-driven workshop practices; and Displaying "zero-tolerance." Ethic violations don't occur very often at the Pole. But when they do, I take swift and deliberate action. I stop the offense, conduct an investigation, and initiate the appropriate consequences. (5, para:71)

> Awareness is knowing what is going on, under, over, around, and through you. The ability to

monitor, with accuracy, the behaviors of others is acquired—and is a lifetime pursuit. (7:16)

Here are some thoughts for consideration regarding implementing effective managerial oversight and evaluation processes within the organization:

1. To be very detail oriented in all aspects of the management of the organization no matter how high up in the organization's ladder

    One of the biggest benefits of being Santa Claus is the fact that I'm on "the point." Although most everyone works his or her little ears and antlers off to make sure our mission is accomplished, I'm the one usually in the spotlight. (5:52)

    It has been my observation over the years that nations, tribes and lesser bands rise and fall on the strength of their leaders and on the ability with which their leaders carry out the responsibilities of office... Chieftains and subordinate leaders must learn the responsibilities of their office. Without such knowledge, how can they fulfill their duties? (10, para:60–62)

Important components to consider when developing an implementation plan for being aware of, researching, and practicing all aspects of the management of the organization should include the following: (1) Managing self: integrity/honesty, interpersonal skills, continual learning, resilience, oral communication, written communication, flexibility, and problem-solving. (2) Managing projects: team building, customer service, technical credibility, accountability, decisiveness, and influencing. (3) Managing people: human capital management, leveraging diversity, conflict management, public service motivation, and devel-

oping others. (4) **Managing programs: technology management, financial management, creativity/innovation, partnering, and political savvy. (5) Leading organizations: external awareness, vision, strategic thinking, and entrepreneurship (fsa.usda.gov).**

2. To take formal trips down into the depths of the organization to view and maintain an awareness of its everyday workings

   Now I ask for (and listen to) the elves' ideas and opinions on most everything we do. I even let them make many of the toy-making decisions we face. And the production line has never run better. (5:37)

   We really do look forward to your regular visits to the shop floor. We like it when you stop to chat with each of us to see how things are going. It hasn't been that way, but that doesn't matter. It's that way now, and we're grateful that it is. (5:41)

   Managers regularly exhort employees to do their best. Many workers lack an awareness of what "best" might be. The effective manager engages in periodic pulse-taking efforts. Any departure between tasks self-perceived and tasks performed can be identified and resolved. (7:97)

   You can observe a lot by just watching. (Yogi Berra, Former New York Yankee "Hall of Fame" baseball player)

Important components to consider when developing an implementation plan for management to utilize walking around to keep an awareness of everyday workings should include the following: (1) Develop a positive attitude toward and place, as a

priority, the need to frequently "get out" into the organization to increase awareness of employees, both regarding their professional responsibilities and personal life (i.e., as much as they wish to share). (2) Place on your weekly schedule, varying the days and times of the day from week to week, to informally walk around to develop a closer relationship with employees. (3) Have ready some prepared questions in advance to ask employees that are related to their job and personal life (i.e., as much as they wish to share). (4) Be prepared to be a good listener and to accept employee input as presented. (5) Review all employee input and consider using the input as part of your assessment regarding the need for organizational change and improvement. (6) Give employees feedback regarding overall trends related to their cumulative concerns and recommendations (Richard A. Pazasis, Retired Executive and Author of *Guide to Becoming an Effective Manager: Thoughts for Consideration*)

3. To develop and implement formal monitoring, assessment, and evaluation processes related the organization's vision, mission, goals, objectives, and strategies, to ensure the continued evaluation of the entire organization for the purpose of organizational improvement and success, and to formally publish and disseminate evaluations of the organization's progress toward goal achievement utilizing internal and external audit results

    Both a concern for performance and a concern for people are essential. A highly adaptive organization is characterized by managers who serve, equally well, both the corporate and collegial functions. (7:20)

    Evaluation is a critical aspect of all successful programs and projects. Benefits of a comprehensive evaluation process include, but are not limited to, ensure your organization projects/programs are aligned with mission objectives; enable your organization to learn, confirm, and improve the services and products you provide to participants, communities, and customers; and improves program processes and contributes to cost-effectiveness in activities. (First Nations Development Institute)

Important components to consider when developing an implementation plan for developing and implementing general organization-wide monitoring, assessment, and evaluation processes should include the following: (1) Implement periodic in-house formal monitoring, assessment, and evaluation processes if you are a start-up or small-size organization, or contract out with reputable audit companies or consultants if you are a medium- to large-size organization, related to periodically assessing and evaluating the organization's progress toward reaching its stated vision, mission, goals, objectives, and strategies. (2) Use the following as headings when developing criteria for assessing an organization: effectiveness in the achievement of all outcomes related the organization's stated mission and goals, efficiency used in reaching the stated mission and goals, quality of outcomes related to the mission and goals, time liness in reaching the desired mission and goals, financial support provided to attain the mission and goals, and workplace environment resulting from policies and processes implemented to reach the mission and goals. (3) Consider the organization's financial and legal viability/compliance and the organization's internal and external communication systems as your first priority for monitoring, assessment, and evaluation. (4) Accept, publish, communicate, and utilize the results to inform all stakeholders and to, as soon as possible, develop action plans that create organizational improvements as quickly as possible (Richard A. Pazasis, retired executive and author of *Guide to Becoming an Effective Manager: Thoughts for Consideration*).

4. To develop a specific employee evaluation processes and appropriate evaluation instruments that periodically assess and communicate employee performance against expectations found on each employee's job description

    Job evaluation seeks to provide equity by an internal alignment of job values. Performance appraisal provides a basis for both rewards and other actions such as coaching. Modern appraisal philosophy focuses on goals and mutual goal setting, and the most popular approach for higher-level jobs is management by objectives... (4:481)

    Organizations still need to have a performance management process. Performance management is a way to provide feedback, accountability, and documentation for performance outcomes. (Sharlyn Lauby, management consultant and author)

Important components to consider when developing an implementation plan for an organization-wide employee evaluation process should include the following: Management Involvement—where managers are responsible for setting performance expectations, providing feedback, and coaching. Goal Setting—where managers and assigned employees mutually establish goals that are aligned with job descriptions. Learning and Development—once goals are set, employees need to have the knowledge and skills to do the work with management investing in employee learning and development. Feedback and Coaching—employees want to know how they are performing because they want to do a good job, so managers need to regularly tell employees about their performance regarding what's good and what could be improved. Ongoing Conversation—management should create a culture that supports ongoing discussions about

performance, goals, learning, coaching, etc. (Sharlyn Lauby, Author of "5 Key Components of Any Successful Performance Management Process," June 27, 2017, para: hrbartender.com).

5. To clearly communicate, directly to each employee, the results of evaluating the achievement of their performance expectations and acknowledge and reward successful employee performance

I regularly meet with the elves and reindeer to discuss their performance, share my observations, and reemphasize the importance of integrity-driven workshop practices. (5:71)

Today, feedback is regarded as essential for personal growth. Certain characteristics of feedback should prevail. It should be non-judgmental, positive, reciprocal, useful, timely, and objective. (7:25)

Important components to consider when developing an implementation plan for the specific acknowledgment and rewarding of employee success should include the following: (1) Positive behavior is best encouraged through positive reinforcement, rather than through negative consequences, which encourages the repetition of positive behavior. (2) Positive reinforcement is most successful when applied when the employee is closest to performing the desired behavior. (3) Both continuous (i.e., after each desired behavior is totally exhibited) and partial (i.e., after each desired behavior is partially exhibited) reinforcements are effective in shaping desired behaviors. (4) Using various interval and ratio schedules for reinforcement should be considered, such as using reinforcements on a fixed interval (i.e., usually on a fixed time period) or on a variable interval (i.e., usually on a random time period) and on a fixed ratio (i.c., after a fixed number of correct responses) or on a variable ratio (i.e., after a variable number of correct responses) (4, para:69–74).

6. To always be aware of the high achievers within the organization and allocate time to reinforce all high achievers (e.g., increase their involvement, advance them in position when appropriate, recognize their achievements throughout the organization utilizing both monetary and nonmonetary rewards, make them role models and mentors)

    Managers should be certain that all employee contributions, both large and small, are recognized. (2:51)

    Your super stars earned their way…by exhibiting consistently outstanding performance. And I used to think the best thing I could do for those folks was to leave them alone and let them do their thing. Boy was I wrong. Like everyone else, great performers don't like to be ignored or taken for granted. Even though some may not admit publically, in private most realize that they need to be worked with, involved, recognized, and rewarded. (5:64)

    One of the characteristics of a leader so often missing in action is his willingness to encourage the growth of subordinates. The true leader not only keeps his people growing on the job (staff development), but also rising in the organization (career development). (7:30)

    My father had a simple test that helps me measure my own leadership quotient [management success]: "When you are out of the office," he once asked me, "does your staff carry on remarkably well without you? (Martha Peek, retired super-intendent of schools, Mobile County School Department, Alabama)

The best leader [manager] is the one who has sense enough to pick good men to do what he wants done, and the self-restraint to keep from meddling with them while they do it. (Theodore Roosevelt, twenty-sixth president of the United States)

Important components to consider when developing an implementation plan for focusing on high-achieving employees: (1) Get them involved in decision-making, strategy setting, procedure development, and problem-solving. (2) Delegate extensively and avoid "micromanaging" them. (3) Encourage them to teach and mentor others, including me. (4) Celebrate their accomplishments and successes. (5) Provide them with highly-specialized training and other career growth opportunities. (6) Show interest in their work and their lives away from work. (7) Hold their coworkers accountable for doing their jobs so that the superstars don't have to pick up the slack. (8) Avoid punishing them for good performance: "You did such a good job handling that mess. The next time we get one, we'll give it to you again" (5:65).

7.   To identify and motivate average employees (e.g., build up their confidence through positive reinforcement for achievements, provide frequent feedback on their performances, provide them with mentors as role models)

Receiving recognition for achievements is one of the most fundamental of human needs. It... reinforces their accomplishments, helping ensure there will be more of them. Effective recognition should take place both day-to-day and through formal programs. Both are important. (2:51)

The middle star group is the backbone of our workshop. They're good, solid workers who, day-in and day-out, bring our mission to life. And many of them have either positive or negative potential to experience super-stardom, while others run the risk of slipping into the falling star ranks. (5:62)

Strong chieftains stimulate and inspire the performance of their Huns. (10:107)

Important components to consider when developing an implementation plan for focusing on average achieving employees: (1) making sure that everyone knows and understands the performance expectations that come from employment; (2) providing training and resources they need to meet those expectations; (3) giving frequent and specific feedback on how they're doing; (4) identifying any obstacles they may be facing, and then doing your best to eliminate those barriers; (5) teaching them how to set, manage, and achieve goals; (6) helping them learn from mistakes and successes; and (7) hooking them up with mentors from the superstar employee ranks (5:63).

8. To identify consistent poor performers and employees who do not comply with company rules and regulations, in attempt to help these performers improve or dismiss them if they do not improve within a reasonable period of time, since avoidance and/or slow reactions to problems usually result in a crisis

For many years it was assumed that high satisfaction leads to high employee performance, but this assumption is not correct. Satisfied workers may be high or low, or only average producers. (4:84)

Preventive discipline is action taken to encourage employees to follow standards... The basic objective is to encourage employee self-discipline. Corrective discipline is an action that follows infraction of a rule; it seeks to discourage further infractions so that future acts will be in compliance with standards. Corrective action requires attention to due process, which means that procedures show concern for the rights of the employee involved... Discipline should be imposed with warning and should be immediate, consistent, and impersonal. (4, para:317–318)

I don't know about you, but for me, the one aspect of leadership that I find most difficult and distasteful is dealing with employee performance problems. Don't really care for it. But since occasional problems are inevitable, and since it is the leader's job to address them, this is an area that I've really worked on. (5, para:60)

Criticism is an essential component of any response system. It is part evaluation. It is part feedback. It is part of a two-way communication loop. (7:34)

All managers must exercise some degree of effective control over their subordinates. Despite all the preventative measures designated to anticipate aberrant behavior, corrective action must sometimes be taken. Some managers cannot constructively criticize others in fear of being disliked, will not criticize through defiance, or do not criticize because of apathy. The manager who fails to take appropriate action as expected by his organization should himself be placed on the back burner. (7, para:47)

A Hun's performance does not always result in desired performance. (10:106)

If you tell a Hun he is doing a good job when he isn't, he will not listen long and, worse, will not believe praise when it is justified. (10:109)

Important components to consider when developing an implementation plan for focusing on poor-performing employees should include the following: (1) Always remember that to rehabilitate an underperforming employee is less costly to an organization than to replace and retrain a new employee. (2) Take immediate notice if an employee is showing signs of continuing to slack off and underperform through the normal implementation of formal performance reviews. (3) Collect and document factual information regarding an employee's underperformance in relationship to the employee's job description, which should include performance responsibilities and expectations. (4) Have a sit-down with the underperforming employee to discuss and review all documented poor performance documentation. (5) Present the underperforming employee with an improvement plan, with time lines for additional formal performance reviews. (6) Offer the underperforming employee support through either additional training or setting him/her up with an in-house mentor. (7) If the underperforming employee show significant improvement, compliment him/her, but continue to carefully evaluate the employee so he/she does not regress. (8) If the employee continues to underperform, begin dismissal procedures (Richard A. Pazasis, Retired Executive and Author of *Guide to Becoming an Effective Manager: Thoughts for Consideration*).

Managerial Improvement Chart

egend: Within every category, circle, whether you feel each subcategory skill is a strength (S) or a weakness (W). Then, if the subcategory is a weakness, next to each subcategory skill, circle your progress toward improvement as follows: I, initiated; IP, in progress; S, strength.

Remember: It is important to keep areas of strength strong while, over time, being patient to improve all weak areas.

Leadership means having ultimate responsibility and account-ability for successfully carrying out the purpose (i.e., mission) and expectations (i.e., goals) of an organization by selecting, training, supporting, motivating, and steering employees in a direction that creates and sustains a successful organization.

1. To be visible and visibly proud of your organization, both internally and externally, and to be its number one cheerleader
   S or W / I or IP or S

2. To consistently convey your organization's vision, mission, and goals through writings, at meetings, during presenta-tions, and when making decisions
   S or W / I or IP or S

3. To spend time communicating effectively with both employees and clients, and within both the formal and informal social structures of the organization (i.e., be visi-ble and practice effective two-way communication), so all involved with the organization will feel like partners and

continually link with, contribute toward, and support the successful achievement of the organization
S or W / I or IP or S

4. To be accessible, considerate, respectful, and supportive to all constituents (i.e., employees and clients) and develop positive relationships and perceptions through consistent communication and modeling by treating people right, keeping promises, standing for what is right in decision-making, and always telling the truth
S or W / I or IP or S

5. To be skillful regarding bringing about change by not pushing events before their time, complimenting individuals regarding their past and present efforts and achievements, introducing new challenges and explaining in detail why change is needed and the potential benefits, allowing for discussion and reflection and even discourse, soliciting ideas for implementation of change and possible alternatives, identifying resources necessary for success, and always remaining patient throughout any change process
S or W / I or IP or S

6. To spend time teaching and mentoring all employees (i.e., fostering organizational knowledge and experiential learning) regarding the main components necessary for organizational success and adapting to change
S or W / I or IP or S

7. To see that employees are treated fairly, appreciated for the positive difference they make with recognition for their contributions with the use of positive rather than negative reinforcement whenever possible and to work within an organizational environment climate that they can be comfortable in and proud of
S or W / I or IP or S

8. To develop, over time, a win-win and healthy partnership-type organizational climate that advocates for moving toward a more "flat-type" span of managerial organizational structure with a more participative win-win

managerial decision-making process and also focusing on employee personal health and happiness, even within large organizations
S or W / I or IP or S

9. To accept the position of leadership with the responsibility and willingness to create a positive organizational culture through shared values
S or W / I or IP or S

10. To be courageous when doing your job and making decisions by always doing what is right and what is ethical
S or W / I or IP or S

Organization means to be successful, every organization must have a clear organizational structure that is documented and communicated. At a minimum, the structure should include a chart or diagram of its main components (i.e., divisions of personnel and work functions) and how they are connected, including sets of relationships between employees and their job assignments to meet the organization's vision, mission, and goals.

1. To chart out (i.e., in a flowchart or diagram) the organization's structure, which may include, but not be limited to, levels and connections between departments, personnel, job functions, and communication links that tie the main components required to accomplish the organization's vision, mission, and goals
S or W / I or IP or S

2. To make clear each employee's connection and role to the organization with written job descriptions (i.e., position title, qualifications, job responsibilities, salary and benefits, and performance expectations)
S or W / I or IP or S

3. To staff (i.e., identify, appoint, and retain) the organization with only qualified employees not only who will be an excellent fit within the organization but also who will help

and not hinder the organization's achievement toward its vision, mission, and goals
S or W / I or IP or S

4. To describe in writing (i.e., in a brochure format), publish, and disseminate, both internally and externally, the organization's official mission, goals, rules, procedures, programs, and services
S or W / I or IP or S

Goals means achievable goals, with specific objectives and strategies leading to the implementation of each goal, are the road map to an organization's success. They need to be related directly to the organization's vision and mission, they need to be doable with the appropriation of resources to ensure success, and they need to be communicated.

1. To include representation (i.e., participative management) from a variety of stakeholders, from both within and without the organization when developing the organization's goals, objectives, and strategies
S or W / I or IP or S

2. To develop, in an action plan format, goals, objectives, and strategies that can be delivered (i.e., they are doable) and that can be broken down into manageable parts, including *what* needs to be accomplished, *why* it needs to be accomplished, *when* does it need to be accomplished, *who* will be involved in its accomplishment, *how* will it be accomplished, *what* resources will be needed to ensure its accomplishment, and *how* will its progress be measured
S or W / I or IP or S

3. To build in benchmark time lines for the ongoing measurement and evaluation of all goals, objectives, and strategies to track progress and to reassess and allow flexibility for appropriate changes as needed to ensure maximum achievement (i.e., to ensure that the goals, objectives, and

strategies remain valid and doable in light of changing conditions)
S or W / I or IP or S

Communication means organizations will not be successful without effective communication. Communication is the glue that keeps all of the main components of the organization together. When the glue remains strong and intact, all components remain firmly bonded, and the organization withstands erosion. But when the glue erodes, the organization weakens until the glue is replaced with new glue. For communication to be effective, it must be two-way (i.e., sending as well as receiving information).

1. To communicate with each other as managers to ensure consistent communication throughout the organization
    S or W / I or IP or S
2. To make certain that all types of communication disseminated throughout the organization, both written and verbal, are clear and are understood by the expected recipients
    S or W / I or IP or S
3. To develop various procedures to listen to employees and clients and include them in assessing the implementation of the organization's vision, mission, goals, objectives, and strategies and leadership effectiveness and to seek and use feedback from employees and clients through managerial visibility and other means (e.g., walking around, meetings, surveys, telephone calls, e-mails, open office, advisory groups)
    S or W / I or IP or S
4. To walk in the employees' shoes from time to time by going into the trenches of your organization to experience various employee roles
    S or W / I or IP or S
5. To always follow up as quickly as possible regarding responses to questions, concerns, and suggestions
    S or W / I or IP or S

6. To implement periodic formal communication audits of the organization, publish the results, and make necessary improvements as recommended within the audit's findings and recommendations
S or W / I or IP or S

Administration means administrative procedures, processes, and actions must be efficient to ensure the most cost-effective operations related to all aspects of an organization, including that of management and employee interactions. Achieving the organization's vision, mission, goals, objectives, and strategies should include obtaining, providing, and getting the most out of all valuable resources. Especially during times when resources are limited and increasingly more costly to obtain, the organization's administrative processes must be extremely cognizant of its ability to provide the necessary financial support for the organization to be effective in the most prudent manner possible. In addition, the organization is required to ensure that all proper fiduciary responsibilities, such as legal and financial requirements and procedures, are complied with and to clearly keep records of and communicate such procedures as required. And to do all this, management must utilize effective time management skills!

1. To make the most of time as a leader and manager (i.e., every minute that goes by is lost and cannot be recovered), which should include, but not be limited to, prioritizing managerial tasks on a daily and weekly basis, preparing in advance for meetings and seeing that participants in meetings have preliminary information concerning the content of each meeting, keeping meetings on time and on task and allow for two-way communication, only scheduling meetings with agenda topics that cannot be communicated via various nonmeeting processes, utilizing time-saving technology for communication and record keeping, and developing/communicating/implementing effective time management processes throughout the organization
S or W / I or IP or S

116

2. To make the most of employees by involving them in periodic meetings, when appropriate and possible; to solicit input and recommendations regarding the development and implementation of cost-effective organizational policies, processes, and decisions; to increase employee to ensure that proper fiduciary responsibilities, regarding following procedures and keeping accurate and required records related to all legal and financial requirements, are complied with; and to keep on file such records related to such responsibilities and procedures and make such records available upon request or when required to file with the appropriate agencies
    S or W / I or IP or S
3. To ensure that proper fiduciary responsibilities, regarding following procedures and keeping accurate and required records to all legal and financial requirements, are complied with and to keep on file such records related to such responsibilities and procedures and make such records available upon request or when required to file with the appropriate agencies
    S or W / I or IP or S
4. To implement discount/bulk/cooperative purchasing practices, the soliciting of price quotes (i.e., bids) from reliable sources, the incorporation of a paper reduction and recycling program, and the reduction of postage and shipping costs, whenever possible
    S or W / I or IP or S
5. To take advantage of all local, state, and federal incentives to start up or relocate and operate
    S or W / I or IP or S
6. To utilize technology whenever possible for communication, production, publishing, and record keeping, with a dual backup data and record-keeping storage system at an alternate site to protect all valuable data and records (e.g., backup disks, cloud technology), which will allow management to spend more time on higher-impact responsibilities
    S or W / I or IP or S

7. To utilize facilities, materials, and equipment efficiently and effectively, institute a preventive maintenance program for facilities and equipment, implement a periodic equipment replacement program, and provide needed services and supplies for indoor and outdoor facility cleanliness and general upkeep
S or W / I or IP or S

8. To implement cross-training of employees to ensure that there are at least two employees who can perform the same job in case an employee is either temporarily or permanently unable to perform his or her job responsibilities and to develop, among all employees, an appreciation and understanding concerning how all workers are interdependent in achieving the organization's mission
S or W / I or IP or S

Management means coordinated oversight and evaluation is a very important component of effective management and must include monitoring the entire organization on a regular basis (i.e., knowing what is going on at all levels), establishing and implementing personnel evaluation programs for performance accountability, and measuring and evaluating goal attainment by the organization.

1. To be very detail oriented in all aspects of the management of the organization no matter how high up in the organization's ladder
S or W / I or IP or S

2. To take formal trips down into the depths of the organization to view and maintain an awareness of its everyday workings
S or W / I or IP or S

3. To develop and implement formal monitoring, assessment, and evaluation processes related the organization's vision, mission, goals, objectives, and strategies, to ensure the continued evaluation of the entire organization for the purpose of organizational improvement and success, and to

formally publish and disseminate evaluations of the organization's progress toward goal achievement utilizing internal and external audit results
S or W / I or IP or S

4. To develop a specific employee evaluation processes and appropriate evaluation instruments that periodically assess and communicate employee performance against expectations found on each employee's job description
S or W / I or IP or S

5. To clearly communicate, directly to each employee, the results of evaluating the achievement of their performance expectations and acknowledge and reward successful employee performance
S or W / I or IP or S

6. To always be aware of the high achievers within the organization and allocate time to reinforce all high achievers (e.g., increase their involvement, advance them in position when appropriate, recognize their achievements throughout the organization utilizing both monetary and nonmonetary rewards, make them role models and mentors)
S or W / I or IP or S

7. To identify and motivate average employees (e.g., build up their confidence through positive reinforcement for achievements, provide frequent feedback on their performances, provide them with mentors as role models)
S or W / I or IP or S

8. To identify consistent poor performers and employees who do not comply with company rules and regulations, in attempt to help these performers improve or dismiss them if they do not improve within a reasonable period of time, since avoidance and/or slow reactions to problems usually result in a crisis
S or W / I or IP or S

Bibliography

Brown, Dan. *Origin.* New York: Anchor Books / Random House, 2017.

Burke, Ronald J., and Cary L. Cooper. *Building More Effective Organizations.* United Kingdom: Cambridge University Press, 2008.

Covey, Stephen R. *The 7 Habits of Highly Effective People: Powerful Lessons in Personal Change.* New York: Simon & Schuster, 1990.

Davis, Keith. *Human Behavior at Work: Organizational Behavior.* New York: McGraw-Hill Book Company, 1981.

Harvey, Eric, David Cottrell, Al Lucia, and Mike Hourigan. *The Leadership Secrets of Santa Claus.* Dallas: Performance Systems Corporation, 2003.

Mackenzie, Alec. *The Time Trap.* New York: American Management Association, 1990.

Maidment, Robert. *Robert's Rules of Disorder: A Guide to Mismanagement.* Louisiana: Pelican Publishing Company, 1976.

Merriam-Webster's Dictionary and Thesaurus. Springfield, MA: Merriam-Webster Inc., 2014.

Randel, Jim. *The Skinny on Time Management.* Connecticut: Rand Media Company, 2010.

Roberts, Wess. *Leadership Secrets of Attila the Hun.* New York: Warner Books, 1989.

Untermeyer, Louis. *The Road Not Taken: A Selection of Robert Frost's Poems.* New York: Henry Holt and Company, 1985.

About the Author

Richard A. Pazasis is the NABE 2020 Pinnacle Book Award Winner in the Business Category for his book/textbook: GUIDE TO BECOMING AN EFFECTIVE MANAGER: "Thoughts for Consideration." He retired early as the results of over forty years of successful management experience within both private and public organizations. He holds three earned degrees: two from Northeastern University, Boston, MA, and one from the University of Southern California, Los Angeles, CA, including two with a focus on Administration. He also completed advanced coursework in Management within the Certificate of Special Studies Program at Harvard University, Cambridge, MA, the Doctoral Administration Program at the University of Massachusetts, Amherst, MA, and several advanced management workshops, including "Total Quality Management" training provided by Bentley College, the Foxboro Company, and the Polaroid Corporation. In addition to his formal education and management experience at many organizational levels, he has privately mentored several individuals wishing to earn a certification in Administration, has taught a C.A.G.S. graduate course in Administration for a State University, and has been the lead consultant for several teams evaluation organizations within the New England area, including preparing the final evaluation reports and recommended improvement plans. His passion for helping others to gain the knowledge and skills necessary to become an effective manager has resulted in his authorship of this very unique publication.

CPSIA information can be obtained
at www.ICGtesting.com
Printed in the USA
BVHW080729090220
571842BV00002B/230

9 781647 014094